Encounters with Jesus

Encounters with Jesus

Studies in the Gospel of John

Frances Taylor Gench

Westminster John Knox Press
LOUISVILLE • LONDON

Scripture quotations, unless otherwise indicated, are from the New Revised Standard Version of the Bible, copyright © 1989 by the Division of Christian Education of the National Council of the Churches of Christ in the U.S.A., and used by permission.

Several chapters in this book are revised and enlarged studies of material originally written by Frances Taylor Gench for the 2000–2001 *Horizons* Bible Study, titled "Women and the Word: Studies in the Gospel of John." Used here by permission of the publisher, Presbyterian Women, Presbyterian Church (U.S.A.).

Quotations from Gail R. O'Day's "The Gospel of John" in *The New Interpreter's Bible,* vol. 9 (Nashville, TN: Abingdon Press, 1995), are used by permission of Abingdon Press.

Quotations from Brad H. Young's "Save the Adulteress! Ancient Jewish *Responsa* in the Gospels?" in *New Testament Studies,* 41: 59–70 (1995), © Cambridge University Press, are used by permission of Cambridge University Press.

Quotations from *Johannine Faith and Liberating Community* (Louisville, KY: Westminster/John Knox Press, 1988) by David Rensberger are used by permission of Westminster John Knox Press.

Quotations from *Written That You May Believe: Encountering Jesus in the Fourth Gospel* (New York: Crossroad, 2003) by Sandra M. Schneiders are used by permission of the Crossroad Publishing Company.

Book design by Drew Stevens

First edition
Published by Westminster John Knox Press
Louisville, Kentucky

This book is printed on acid-free paper that meets the American National Standards Institute Z39.48 standard. ♾

PRINTED IN THE UNITED STATES OF AMERICA

07 08 09 10 11 12 13 14 15 16—10 9 8 7 6 5 4 3 2

Library of Congress Cataloging-in-Publication Data

Gench, Frances Taylor.
    Encounters with Jesus : studies in the Gospel of John / Frances Taylor Gench.
      p. cm.
    Includes bibliographical references.
    ISBN-13: 978-0-664-23006-7 (alk. paper)
    ISBN-10: 0-664-23006-7 (alk. paper)
    1. Bible. N.T. John—Criticism, interpretation, etc.   I. Title.

BS2615.52.G46 2007
226.5'07—dc22   2006052990

FOR MY FATHER

David W. A. Taylor

Contents

Acknowledgments

This book has grown out of my teaching of the Gospel of John, and thus conversations in a variety of classrooms have had an immeasurable influence upon it. Students at Gettysburg Lutheran Seminary and Union-PSCE in Richmond, Virginia, have been my primary conversation partners, and I am thankful for the privilege of engaging biblical texts daily with such faithful, intelligent, and interesting people, and of even getting paid to do it. I am grateful to Presbyterian Women for the opportunity to author the 2000–2001 *Horizons* Bible Study on the Gospel of John and for conversations with women throughout the Presbyterian Church (U.S.A.) during that year. The New York Avenue Presbyterian Church in Washington, D.C., has also been a lively forum for discussion of all the texts featured in this book, and its pastor, Roger J. Gench, inspires me with remarkable preaching of them. Last but not least, I am grateful to the administration and trustees of Union-PSCE for a sabbatical leave on which to work on this project, and to Stephanie Egnotovich and Daniel Braden of Westminster John Knox Press for their meticulous shepherding of it from beginning to end.

This book is dedicated to my father, David W. A. Taylor, who was in conversation with me about the Bible well before I could read, and who has patiently reviewed every thought I have had about the Gospel of John, providing masterful editorial commentary every step of the way.

Frances Taylor Gench
Richmond, Virginia

Introduction

What is your favorite Gospel: Matthew, Mark, Luke, or John? Martin Luther, the father of the Protestant Reformation, made no bones about his own preference. In his "Preface to the New Testament," Luther wrote, "John's Gospel is the one, fine, true, and chief gospel, and is far, far to be preferred over the other three and placed high above them."[1] John Calvin, another great Protestant Reformer and my own patron saint, also had special appreciation for the Gospel of John. In his commentary on John, Calvin wrote, "I am accustomed to say that this Gospel is a key to open the door for understanding the rest; for whoever shall understand the power of Christ, as it is here strikingly portrayed, will afterwards read with advantage what the others relate about the Redeemer who was manifested."[2] But Calvin and Luther were not alone in their regard for John; in many respects it has been the Gospel most beloved by the whole church.

The reason why many people have had a special love for the Gospel of John is its Christology, its portrait of Jesus Christ. John is the most consistently christocentric of the Gospels, that is, when we read it, the person and promises of Jesus Christ seem more immediate and available. Jesus seems up close and personal in John and we find ourselves in direct encounter with him. And there is a very good reason for that, too: Jesus talks constantly in John! He is exceedingly verbal. Recently I heard someone describe Jesus in the Gospel of John this way: "Wordy is the Lamb!" It is not a bad description, for Jesus, in John, does not habitually speak in brief sayings or parables, as in the other Gospels; nor does he have much to say about the kingdom of God or the moral behavior expected of his followers. Instead, in unusually extended dialogues, and occasionally in monologues, he talks about himself. His divine identity is no secret, and he does not urge silence upon those who discern it—in contrast to the Gospel of Mark, for example, where Jesus is constantly saying "Shut up!" and "Don't tell anybody!" In the Gospel of John, Jesus speaks quite openly and repeatedly about who he is and what his coming means for the life of the world. Indeed, he speaks far more than he acts and performs fewer wondrous works than in the other Gospels, though the few he does perform are more spectacular.

When I received my first Bible, it was one of those red-letter editions in which all the words of Jesus are printed in red. If you, too, are in possession of such a Bible, then you have probably noticed that there is more red in this Gospel than in any other. Wordy *is* the Lamb! We hear more words come directly out of Jesus' mouth, and they are among the most familiar in all of Scripture: "I am the bread of life. . . . I am the light of the world. . . . I am the good shepherd. The good shepherd lays down his life for the sheep. . . . I am the resurrection and the life. . . . I am the way, and the truth and the life. . . . Do not let your hearts be troubled . . . in my Father's house there are many dwelling places. If it were not so, would I have told you that I go to prepare a place for you? . . . I am the vine, you are the branches. Those who abide in me and I in them bear much fruit. . . . This is my commandment, that you love one another as I have loved you." There are no parallels for any of these familiar words in the other Gospels.

I would be willing to wager that even those people who worship regularly on Sunday mornings at "Her Mattress by the Springs"—even the most casual churchgoers—have probably learned John 3:16 in Sunday school (if not there, then on *Monday Night Football*). They have probably been comforted at funerals by words like "Let not your hearts be troubled" and found hope in Jesus' promise, "I am the resurrection and the life." Because the Gospel of John's language is simple and engaging, lending itself to easy memorization and recall, it also seems to be our most frequent New Testament source of material for billboards, bumper stickers, and pamphlets distributed on street corners and in grocery store parking lots. John is the stuff that bumper stickers are made of. As a result, John has had not only a lot of use but also a lot of abuse by the obnoxious.

There is room for all to engage this intriguing and beloved Gospel, whether one is new to Bible study or a seasoned veteran. Its language is simple and elegant, yet plumbs astonishing depths. Indeed, John has been memorably, although anonymously, described as "a book in which a child can wade and an elephant can swim."[3] Whatever your level of aquatic experience with the Bible, I hope this book will prompt you to jump in.

My aim is to provide an opportunity for you to immerse yourself, alone or in the company of others, in the study of John's Gospel and thereby become better acquainted with the distinctive vision that it represents. Each of the four Gospels provides a distinctive witness to Jesus Christ. From its earliest history, the church has treasured and safeguarded the fact that it has one gospel in four editions—four very different portraits of Jesus to expand and enrich its reflection on his significance for Christian life, faith, and renewal. Still, three of those Gospels, for all their differences, are interrelated: Matthew, Mark, and Luke share certain similarities in outline, contents, order, and wording, and are thus called "Synoptic" (which means that they "see together"). John, however, is in a class by itself. It has been aptly described as the "maverick" Gospel,[4] for its perspective runs free of those found in Matthew, Mark, and Luke. It is the decidedly nonconformist Gospel of the bunch. For this reason, the Gospel of John requires some special study on our part.

Moving from the Synoptic Gospels into the Gospel of John, we enter a very different landscape. The scenery is not entirely unfamiliar, for all four Gospels narrate events related to the life, ministry, death, and resurrection of Jesus Christ. Still, the Gospel of John is remarkably different from the others in its ordering, selection, and interpretation of the events, and most notably in its portrayal of Jesus, who speaks and acts in a highly distinctive manner. For all of these reasons and more, when we enter John we find ourselves in very different surroundings—in a Gospel with a unique perspective on the life and ministry of Jesus Christ. It offers each of us the opportunity to discover (or rediscover) Jesus for ourselves[5]—to dust the cobwebs off of staid or static images of him that may hang in the closets of our minds and enter into renewed and deepened encounter with the vital one who shares with us God's own life.

This book was written with a variety of readers in mind, ordained and lay. I hope that it will be a resource for preachers and teachers who engage the texts on a regular basis in the practice of ministry. It is also designed for use by laypersons and groups interested in substantive Bible study. I present technical matters in an accessible fashion and include study questions with each chapter to facilitate group discussion or individual reflection. In the chapters that follow, we will not consider every passage in John's Gospel, but we will immerse ourselves in study of thirteen central texts that are featured prominently in the church's lectionary and life. I hope that each chapter will facilitate engagement with these texts and reflection on the implications they bear for Christian life, faith, and renewal.

QUESTIONS FOR DISCUSSION OR REFLECTION

Which is your favorite Gospel: Matthew, Mark, Luke, or John,
and why?

How would you describe your relationship with the Gospel of
John and your experience with it? Where have you encountered it?

When you think of the Gospel of John, what favorite verses,
images, or characters come to mind?

Do you know John 3:16 by memory? If so, when did you first
encounter it?

What impressions of the Gospel of John do you bring to your
study of it? To date, what questions has it raised for you?

1

The Word Became Flesh

John 1:1–18

The Gospel of John's distinctive landscape emerges in its opening verses. Entering it, we find that we are not at the banks of the river Jordan, where Mark begins with the story of the adult Jesus' baptism by John (Mark 1). Neither are we in Bethlehem years earlier, in the company of Luke's shepherds or Matthew's magi, pondering the birth of the holy child (Matt. 1–2; Luke 1–2). John pushes the beginning of the story back further still, transporting us to the dawn of time. We have stepped onto a cosmic plane. Fortunately, a road map is provided for our travel[1]—a hymnic prologue (John 1:1–18) that becomes a lens through which we are to read John's entire Gospel.

"IN THE BEGINNING WAS THE WORD . . ."

"In the beginning" God created the heavens and the earth by uttering a word (Gen. 1:1–3). John's opening verses take us back to that beginning and give a glimpse behind the curtains of creation: "In the beginning was the Word, and the Word was with God, and the Word was God. He was in the beginning with God" (1:1–2). From the outset, we are given to understand that we have entered a Gospel narrative of cosmic scope and significance. Although it will be the story of a human being in history, at the same time it will be the story of one who comes from beyond the world and from the beginning of all existence—the

1

story of one who preexisted with God before creation. That eternal one, referred to as the "Word" (*Logos* in Greek), was distinct from God and in communion "with God," yet also identified with God ("was God"). This profound mystery, which is confessed rather than explained, gives expression to the early Christian community's ever-deepening reflection on the absolute significance of Jesus Christ: "Christ is so important that he could not simply have come into being like any other person or object."[2]

Thereupon follows another affirmation that is equally profound: "All things came into being through him, and without him not one thing came into being" (1:3). In other words, the preexistent Christ/Word is the agent of divine creation as well as redemption. Surely this affirmation, too, arises from early Christian conviction about the absolute significance of Christ for human life: "So fundamental to the sense and purpose of existence is the revelation in Christ that he must be conceived as the shaping force in the very beginnings of existence!"[3] Moreover, it has implications for Christian understanding of the world and salvation. We can hardly think of the world as evil, either by origin or nature, for "all things came into being through him." Nor can salvation be envisioned as escape from the world. As Fred Craddock explains: "To think of salvation as basically escape from this world of people and things is to turn one's back on that which God, through Christ, has created. To have a view of salvation that does not embrace all that God created is too small and partial."[4]

Thus begins the Gospel of John—with heady theological affirmations. But John is not primarily concerned with philosophical speculation. What matters most is what the Word means for our lives and for the life of the world. Why? Because "what has come into being in him was life" (v. 4)—the life God intended for us at the very beginning of creation. Hence, that "life was the light of all people" (v. 4)—illumining the meaning and purpose of our lives in relationship to God. In fact, though our travel with John begins on a cosmic plane, we are promptly brought down to the realm of human history (see v. 10), where "the Word became flesh and lived among us" (v. 14). There, in the midst of everyday human reality, the light continues to this day to shine, for "the darkness did not overcome it" (v. 5), though it could also be said that "the darkness did not comprehend it" or "understand" it. John is filled with intriguing wordplays, and the Greek verb *katalambanō* can mean "to overcome," but also "to comprehend." Both may well be in view.

"AND THE WORD BECAME FLESH AND LIVED AMONG US . . ."

The Gospel of John is almost unique in the New Testament in referring to Jesus as the Word or *Logos*.[5] In a day when we find ourselves bombarded with words—literally up to our ears in junk mail, e-mail, and advertising jingles—we may underrate the significance of words. But this was not so in the first century, when words bore sacred power.[6] Indeed, John's description of Jesus as the "Word" or *Logos* would have summoned for them a range of associations. For example, the concept was prominent in a popular Greek philosophy of that time called Stoicism, which held the *logos* to be a sort of cosmic reason—the mind of God that penetrated all things, giving order and structure to the universe. Alternatively, those familiar with the Hebrew Scriptures would surely have associated the "word of the Lord" as both the power of God that called creation into being and the message of God for the human community conveyed by Israel's prophets. Still again, some of the most illuminating associations would have echoed from the Jewish wisdom tradition. In both the Old Testament and later Jewish writings (such as the Apocrypha), an intriguing female figure emerges, Lady Wisdom or Sophia, who is said to have resided with God and to have played a role in creation (Prov. 8); and also to have taken up her dwelling among human beings (Sir. 24), manifesting God's wisdom and glory (Wisd. 7–8). What is one to make of these intriguing parallels? It may well be that the author of John's hymnic prologue deliberately chose a household concept with a wide variety of associations—one that would have appealed to a broad range of both Jewish and Gentile hearers. Moreover, by applying it to Jesus he or she suggested that Jesus fulfilled a vast array of expectations: "The author is saying, in effect: Yes, Christ is all of this—Stoic Logos, Hebrew Bible Word, and Jewish Wisdom—rolled into one person."[7]

This is the staggering claim of John's prologue: the Word has become a person! The eternal one, who is the very self-expression of God, fulfills that function to the full by taking on human flesh: "The Word became flesh and lived among us, and we have seen his glory, the glory as of a father's only son, full of grace and truth" (v. 14). This emphatic affirmation is the hub of John's prologue and the New Testament's boldest expression of Christ's incarnation. It is also at the heart of John's maverick perspective—a difference that may be illustrated in graphic form.[8] If we were to graph the Synoptic Gospels, we would do so horizontally, for Matthew, Mark, and Luke share a horizontal view of God's saving activity:

Synoptic Gospels

creation   prophets   John the Baptist   Jesus

According to the Synoptic presentation, God works in and through history, guiding the world toward a goal. John's Gospel shares aspects of this point of view; indeed, it insists that the Word became flesh in history. But by and large, we would have to graph the Gospel of John vertically, for it sets forth the descent and ascent of the cosmic savior:

Gospel of John

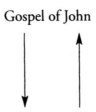

The eternal Word, which became flesh in Jesus of Nazareth, had a previous life with God before he came below—a life that he manifests in human history. Then, at the end of his earthly career, he returns from whence he came. His cross is referred to as the moment in which he is "lifted up" from the earth (3:14; 8:28; 12:32–34)—the moment in which he departs from the world and returns to God and to the glory that was his before creation.

A fascinating image in 1:14 further illustrates this distinctive perspective, though it is often lost in English translation. Most translations convey that the Word became flesh and "lived" or "dwelt" among us, but the Greek verb employed (*eskēnōsen*) is much more graphic. The Word literally "pitched a tent" among us—the Word "camped out" among us. This striking image is significant on two counts. For one thing, it conveys that the Word's residence in the world is temporary—he is on a journey. We are to keep in mind where he came from and where he is going. For another thing, the image calls to mind the tent or tabernacle in which God's glory was present with the Israelites in their wilderness wanderings, long before there was a temple. For John, the implication is plain: Jesus is now the place where God is manifested to humanity, where God's glory is revealed.

"The Word became flesh and 'camped out' among us, and we have seen his glory, the glory as of a father's only son, full of grace and truth" (v. 14). What does this bold affirmation of incarnation mean for our lives and the life of the world? It means that "human beings can see, hear, and know God in ways never before possible"; they are given "intimate, palpable, corporeal access to the cosmic reality of God."[9] Who among us has not longed for such access, for a glimpse of the divine, one little peek at God! The disciple named Philip voices this desire for all of us at a later point in the Gospel of John when he says to Jesus, "Lord, show us the Father, and we shall be satisfied" (14:8). Jesus' response is: Look at me—"Whoever has seen me has seen the Father" (14:9). The prologue concludes on this same note: "No one has ever seen God. It is God the only Son, who is close to the Father's heart, who has made him known" (1:18). Therein lies the Fourth Gospel's central claim, elaborated on every page: Jesus is the fleshed-out truth about God.

The incarnation and the new access to divine reality that it provides are significant in one further respect: it makes possible a new relationship with God. On the one hand, the incarnation binds God to us, in that God did not stay distant from us, but chose to live with us, to know our struggles and to identify with us completely: "To become flesh is to know joy, pain, suffering, and loss. It is to love, to grieve, and someday to die."[10] In the incarnation, God's own self has been bound to everyday human experience.[11] On the other hand, the incarnation binds us to God and to each other in a new and intimate relationship as God's own children. Not all will receive Jesus as the revelation of God's own self or accept the gift of life he offers (see vv. 10–11), and therein lies the tragic dimension of John's story. "But to all who received him, who believed in his name, he gave power to become children of God" (v. 12).

John is convinced that every one of us longs for such an intimate relationship with God. It is significant that the first words out of Jesus' mouth in the Gospel of John are these: "What are you looking for?" (1:38; see also 20:15). This central question of invitation is asked of every one of us who enters John's story, calling us to discern and articulate our deepest longings. To John's way of thinking, the fundamental human longing is for God. Augustine once expressed much the same sentiment when he prayed: "You have made us for yourself, O God, and our hearts are restless still, until they rest in you."[12] Jesus' words of invitation summon us to travel further into John's story in order to grasp more fully the light and life he offers. Now equipped with a road map, a lens with which to read everything that follows, we can take Jesus up on a second invitation, uttered on the heels of the first: "Come and see" (1:39).

CONCLUDING REFLECTIONS

A few concluding reflections may help highlight the distinctive contribution that the Gospel of John makes to our understanding of both Jesus Christ and the God who sent him. There is no denying it: John presents a very high Christology, that is, a portrait of Christ that highlights his divinity and exalted status. At the same time, John insists on Christ's humanity, for "the Word became flesh and lived among us" (1:14). Still, one cannot avoid the impression that Jesus' divinity outshines his humanity in John. Readers may even find themselves wondering if Jesus' feet are really touching the ground.

There is probably a good reason that the evangelist John emphasizes Jesus' divinity more than his humanity: it was likely the focus of intense conflict with the synagogue. Many of the Christians to whom the Gospel of John was first addressed were Jewish Christians who may have been cast out of the synagogue for their confession of faith in Jesus Christ, for there are three explicit references in John to such an experience (9:22, 34; 12:42; 16:2). The matter of Jesus' humanity would not have placed them in conflict with their compatriots, but confession of his divinity surely would have and may account for the fact that the Gospel focuses so heavily on this aspect of Jesus' identity. In short, this is what they were arguing about. The Johannine Christians were so convinced that Jesus was the very revelation of God that they were willing to put themselves on the line for this confession, and having paid a price for it, they were likely to attach special importance to it. Jesus' divinity was subsequently the primary focus of their theological energies and reflection, and their witness to it challenges us, too, to see in Jesus a genuine peek at God (14:8–10).

That John's portrait does not do full justice to Jesus' humanity is not an insurmountable problem. Indeed, this is where the early church's wisdom in preserving one gospel in four very different editions is apparent. The other Gospels, and Mark in particular, amply fill out the portrait of Jesus' humanity (so amply that readers of Mark may wonder if full justice is done to Jesus' divine nature). Thus the four Gospels complement one another, challenging us to consider different aspects of our own confession of faith in Christ.

"Incarnation" is another distinctive feature of John's christological portrait. "Incarnation" means "embodiment in flesh" and refers to the belief that a preexistent divine being (the Word or the Son) entered our world and became human. It has become so much a part of Christian faith that it may occasion surprise to note that only John among the Gospels explicitly bears witness to it. This belief finds expression in a handful of other New Testament texts (Col. 1:15–20; Heb. 1:1–4; Phil. 2:6–11). The Gospel of John, however, provides the fullest and clearest statement of incarnation in the New Testament, and only in John does Jesus himself speak of a previous life with God.

The importance of this contribution should not escape us, for it broadens our perspective on the love of God in Christ. As Raymond Brown points out, "For most of the New Testament God's supreme act of love is embodied in Jesus' self-giving on the cross." The cross is important in John's story, too, as a sign of God's love and of the extent to which love is willing to go. "No one has greater love than this" (15:13). But John also talks about incarnation, which "brings into the picture an earlier act of love: the divine self-giving in becoming one of us."[13] It is, in a sense, a stereoscopic perspective that stretches the horizons of our reflection on the gift of God in Christ.

Brown also points out that the way the evangelist John begins the Gospel says something very important about the way we think about God. He tells a story about a monk from one of the great Eastern non-Christian religious traditions who expressed puzzlement over this Gospel's opening line, "In the beginning was the Word": "Why don't Christians think that in the beginning there was silence? You must have a noisy God!"[14] What Brown goes on to note is that "in a way we do have a noisy God, a God who is outwardly oriented. On the opening page of the Bible, the very first thing we are told about God is that He spoke and things were created."[15] It is striking when you stop and think about it: John does not begin with "In the beginning there was silence" or "In the beginning there was God" but rather with "In the beginning was the Word." What this suggests is that "God's very nature is self-communication, self-opening, self-gift, that is creative of the other."[16]

A final word needs to be said about the Gospel of John's inordinate use of "Father" language for God, as this matter will be of concern to some readers. In recent years, many Christians have become increasingly sensitized to the ways in which the words that roll off our tongues can limit imaginations and understanding of the divine presence in our lives. As the hymn writer Brian Wren reminds us, "language, like tobacco, is habit-forming," and some patterns of our speaking are addictive and may damage both the user and others who breathe the same linguistic air.[17] One of those habits has been exclusive reference to God in male terms. Though the Scriptures use myriad images in referring to God—some masculine, some feminine—it is clear from Scripture that God is above and beyond all human gender. Yet many today, in their prayer and praise, speak of God in exclusively male terms, especially as "Father."

For those who are concerned about inclusive language, the Gospel of John presents a dilemma in that it refers to God as Father far more than any other New Testament document—more than one hundred times. (By comparison, Mark refers to God as Father 4 times; Luke, 15 times; and Matthew, 49 times.) There is no easy solution, but it may help to understand the significance of this language. John's point is *not* that God is male, but rather that God is intimately related to us in Christ. As New Testament scholar Gail O'Day has pointed out, "Father language in John is essentially relational. . . . This language, then, is not primarily the language of patriarchy but is instead the language of intimacy, relationship, and family."[18] It is used not to reinforce patterns of male domination, "but in order to evoke a new world in which intimate relations with God and one another are possible."[19] For this reason, substituting "God" for "Father" is problematic, for it runs the risk of obscuring the relational and familial imagery that is central to John's understanding of what God has made available to us in Christ. Some may wish to substitute the word "Parent," others will not. My own decision as author has been to limit the use of Father language in my own commentary on the text and retain it when quoting from the NRSV (from which all the quotations in this study are taken). This is not an entirely satisfactory solution, but it attempts to respect diversity within a diverse church. Let us be patient and open with one another as we continue to discuss together very real differences of opinion on this important matter, and patient also with the Gospel of John, so that we do not miss the clarity with which it depicts the one who grants us power to become children of God.

QUESTIONS FOR DISCUSSION OR REFLECTION

Have one person do a dramatic reading of John 1:1–18. Following the reading, share briefly: What most captures your attention as you hear the story? What questions does it raise for you?

What echoes of the first five verses of Genesis do you hear in the opening five verses of John? What do you think they suggest about the story John will tell?

In the evangelist's day, many religions taught that salvation entailed escape from the world, or turning one's back on the creation, a view John explicitly counters with testimony to the goodness of creation in 1:3. Have you ever encountered such a view? Is it alive and well in our day?

What do you think about this Gospel's affirmation of the Christ-Word's preexistence and role in creation? Does this affirmation have any bearing on our participation in the life of the world, in your view?

Novelist Frederick Buechner, commenting on John's testimony to the incarnation, observes: "One of the blunders religious people are particularly fond of making is the attempt to be more spiritual than God."[20] What do you think he meant by this? Would you agree with his observation?

Poet and author Kathleen Norris says this about "incarnation": "it reveals the ordinary circumstances of my life to be full of mystery, and gospel, which means 'good news.'"[21] What does incarnation mean to you?

What do you think of the intriguing wordplay in verse 5? The darkness did not "overcome" the light; but maybe it did not "comprehend" it. Both translations are acceptable. Which do you prefer and why?

"What are you looking for?" Imagine a reporter asking this question of passersby on the street. What responses do you think they might give? How would you articulate your own deepest longings? How are they addressed by God in Christ?

John 1:1–18 is frequently read in worship services during the Christmas season. What are your memories of hearing it read? What has it contributed to your Christmas reflection?

As noted, John presents a very high Christology, that is, a portrait of Christ that highlights his divinity and exalted status. At the same time, John insists on Christ's humanity, for "the Word became flesh and lived among us" (1:14). Which affirmation receives greater emphasis in your own theological reflection and faith: Christ's divinity or his humanity? Why, do you think? Which affirmation receives greater emphasis in your community of faith?

Is inclusive language for God an important issue for you? Why, or why not? As you study the Gospel of John, how will you choose to engage John's excessive Father language for God?

What new insights have you gained from your study of John's prologue?

2

Entrance and Exit Points

John 2:1–12 and 19:16–30

The mother of Jesus appears in John's Gospel, but not in association with angels, a manger, swaddling clothes, shepherds, or magi from the East. She is included instead in two scenes that have no parallel in the other Gospels. In John she is present at the inaugural event of Jesus' ministry, at a wedding in Cana (2:1–12); and she reappears at the culminating event of that ministry, at the foot of the cross (19:16–30). These two episodes frame the story of Jesus' public ministry in John and share a web of connections, as we shall see. Indeed, they represent the entrance and exit points in the earthly sojourn of the Word made flesh, and are appropriately considered together.

A WEDDING AT CANA (2:1–12)

Miracle stories are familiar to readers of the four Gospels, filled as they are with extraordinary feats of Jesus in response to desperate human needs—usually needs for healing, food, or safety. But the miraculous act that inaugurates John's account of Jesus' public ministry is puzzling, for no such need is featured there. What is one to make of a story that presents Jesus first and foremost as purveyor of vast quantities of wine? Frankly, some Christians find the episode to be an embarrassing one. (A woman I once met told me that her pastor had assured her that it was unfermented wine.)

On close inspection, other puzzling aspects of the story quickly emerge, evoking more questions than answers. There was a wedding at Cana (we do not know whose) and the mother of Jesus was there, along with Jesus and his disciples, who had also been invited (we do not know why). For some undetermined reason the wine gave out, and Jesus' mother felt compelled to call it to his attention: "They have no wine" (v. 3). Implicit in her words is the suggestion that he can do something about the shortage and thereby avert a social disaster. Jesus, however, responds gruffly to this suggestion: "Woman, what concern is that to you and to me? My hour has not yet come" (v. 4).

Is that any way to speak to your mother? His response (translated literally as "What to me and to you, woman?") employs a Semitic expression with two possible shades of meaning: one conveying hostility ("Get off my back!"), and another disengagement ("This is none of my business"). Most commentators assume the latter in this case. But why does Jesus address his mother as "woman"? Surely no disrespect is intended, for Jesus customarily addresses women in this manner (the Samaritan woman in 4:21, for example, and Mary Magdalene in 20:15). Still, commentators concede that it is a most unusual way for a son to address his mother.

Nonetheless, Jesus' response may well convey a point worth pondering: his freedom from all human controls, even from the claims of his mother.[1] His actions will be governed only by the hour set by God—the hour of the cross (see 7:30; 8:20; 12:23, 27; 13:1; 17:1)—and as he pointedly states, "My hour has not yet come" (v. 4). Nevertheless, his mother persists, directing the servants: "Do whatever he tells you" (v. 5). And despite his clearly stated preference for disengagement in this matter, Jesus then proceeds to address the dilemma at hand. (Go figure!)

But here the narrative slows, pausing to provide extraordinary detail and an indication of where the importance of this story lies: "Now standing there were six stone water jars for the Jewish rites of purification, each holding twenty or thirty gallons. Jesus said to them, 'Fill the jars with water.' And they filled them up to the brim" (vv. 6–7). That the jars were made of stone (rather than clay) ensured the purity of the waters used for the Jewish practice of ceremonial washing before and after meals. That those same jars will soon be filled with wine signifies the emergence of something new in the midst of Judaism.[2] More important, six stone jars containing 20–30 gallons each will soon hold somewhere between 120–180 gallons of wine—an astonishing quantity by any standard. We are given to understand that the miraculous act Jesus is about to perform will be an extravagant one.

That, more than anything else, is what makes this story a suitable introduction to Jesus' ministry in John. Jesus, in John's view, is the giver of extravagant gifts to human beings. He came that we might "have life," and "have it abundantly" (10:10). "From his fullness" we all receive "grace upon grace" (1:16)—through him we are filled to the brim! As John's story unfolds, the nature of the divine gifts that Jesus offers will be explicated; but here at the beginning of Jesus' ministry we are given to understand that they will be lavish beyond our imaginings and of a quality heretofore unknown.

Not everyone will recognize who Jesus is and what he offers. The chief steward, for example, "did not know where [the wine] came from" and could account for the miracle only in human terms: he assumed that the bridegroom had saved the best wine for last (vv. 9–10). The disciples, however, discerned in this miraculous act the very presence of God: "Jesus did this, the first of his signs, in Cana of Galilee, and revealed his glory; and his disciples believed in him" (v. 11).

Miracles, in John, are referred to as "signs," which is to say that their significance lies in that to which they point: the true identity of the one who performed them. What was it about this particular sign that revealed for them the presence of God—of "glory"—in Jesus? Though the story does not spell it out for us, those who carried Old Testament promises in their hearts would have found its meaning quite clear: abundance of wine was one of the consistent Old Testament images for the joy of the messianic "last days" and the arrival of God's new age (see Amos 9:13–14; Joel 3:18; Jer. 31:12; 33:6; Isa. 25:6–10). John affirms that, in the one who provided lavish wine at Cana, the promised day has arrived and God's abundant blessings are poured out upon believers.

AT THE FOOT OF THE CROSS (19:16–30)

John is a consistently christocentric Gospel; everything in it serves to illumine for its readers the identity and significance of Jesus Christ. Thus miraculous "signs" he performs point beyond themselves to some truth about the divine presence at work in him. The same is true of all the characters in the narrative with whom he interacts. Their encounter invariably reveals something of ultimate significance about Jesus. What then do we learn about him from his encounters with his mother?

She is present at the beginning of his public ministry, prompting his first miracle, and then reappears at the foot of the cross, a witness to its end. Oddly enough, in both scenes she is referred to as "the mother of Jesus" rather than by name. As might be expected, these intriguing cameo appearances and references have given rise to a host of symbolic interpretations. Indeed, Beverly Roberts Gaventa notes that "interpretations of Mary in John's Gospel range widely—even wildly."[3] Mary has been viewed variously as representing Judaism, Jewish Christianity, Lady Zion, the new Eve, and the church.

Gaventa herself offers a fresh interpretation of Mary that takes account of the literary contexts in which she appears, as well as John's christocentric focus. Gaventa suggests that "the mother of Jesus" is among John's ways of reminding us that Jesus was a human being.[4] These key references to his mother connect him with human life, a welcome reminder in a Gospel whose portrait of Jesus otherwise underscores his divinity more emphatically than his humanity. In the first chapter of John, Jesus has been introduced as a figure of cosmic significance: the preexistent divine Word, through whom all things were created and will be redeemed—the life and light of the world in whom God's glory is enfleshed—the one who makes God known. Yet at the conclusion of chapter 1 we learn of a father named Joseph and a hometown of Nazareth (1:45–46). And in chapter 2 we are introduced to his mother and brothers (2:12). Thus the appearance of Jesus' mother in 2:1 occurs "within a small network of references to Jesus' relatives and his home. The Logos is not a disembodied spirit, after all, but has family and location just as does any other flesh-and-blood human being. Jesus is simultaneously God's only son and the son of Mary and Joseph."[5]

Mary's reappearance at the foot of the cross is significant for the same reason, for the cross in John is the moment in which the preexistent one is "lifted up" from the earth and returns to his heavenly Father (cf. 3:13–15; 8:28; 12:32–34). Through his death, he returns to a state he has temporarily left during his sojourn in the world. Thus, at the cross, he is separated from all that belongs to his earthly life: "Just as he is stripped of his clothing, he divests himself of his mother and his Beloved Disciple. The human family that is ascribed to him early in the Gospel, and especially at Cana, here is removed at the 'hour' of his return to the Father."[6]

That the mother of Jesus is present at both the inaugural and culminating events of his public ministry links these two scenes, which represent the entrance and exit points in the earthly sojourn of the Word made flesh. Further connections bind these two scenes closer still: the "hour" toward which Jesus pointed at Cana now finally arrives at the cross—the place at which the "glory" present in his ministry from the first comes most fully into view (12:23; 13:31–32; 17:1, 4–5). Ironically, in that hour the giver of choicest, abundant wine is given sour wine to drink. And in that hour, the bearer of divine gifts makes his most extravagant offering: the gift of himself for the life of the world.

At the foot of the cross in John's Gospel, still another divine gift comes into view: the creation of a new family of faith. In his dying moments, Jesus performs the last act of his public ministry as he speaks to his mother and to one who is known to us only as his "Beloved Disciple," and entrusts them to each other: "When Jesus saw his mother and the disciple whom he loved standing beside her, he said to his mother, 'Woman, here is your son.' Then he said to the disciple, 'Here is your mother.' And from that hour the disciple took her into his own home" (19:26–27). These words from the cross give birth to a church, a new family of faith. Here, as elsewhere in the New Testament, the family model that Jesus endorses is that of adoption. Indeed, the words that Jesus speaks from the cross—"Here is your son" and "Here is your mother"—resemble the formulas used for rites of adoption in the ancient world. As Craig Koester observes, "They are appropriate for a scene in which two people, who are connected by their common faith relationship with Jesus rather than by kinship ties, are brought together into relationship with one another, forming the nucleus of a new community."[7]

The import of this adoptive family model for the church ought not to escape us in a day when some voices promote "family values," often proclaiming that only nuclear families ought to be regarded as real families. As family ministry specialist Diana Garland says, a "Christian assumption about families that grows out of the New Testament is that we are to reach beyond the bonds of blood and marriage to embrace others as family." Pointing to John 19 and the creation of the church at the foot of the cross, Garland observes that "the church follows Christ by ensuring that no one in the family of faith is family-less—that everyone is adopted into the family." Indeed, "In the community of faith, people should not be perceived simply in terms of a label like 'single.' Family is more than marital status. The work of the Christian church is to weave every believer into bonds of mutual commitment and love as real as any legal or biological bond recognized by society."[8]

The language of familial intimacy is absolutely central to John's vision of life in Christ. From its opening verses, the Gospel of John proclaims that the Word made flesh came into the world for the express purpose of creating a new family determined by faith: "But to all who received him, who believed in his name, he gave power to become children of God, who were born, not of blood or of the will of the flesh or of the will of man, but of God" (1:12–13). Therein lies good news for many people. As Gail O'Day observes: "People who have no families, who come from destructive families, or who are alienated from their birth families can belong to a new family by virtue of becoming children of God."[9] Jesus promises, "I will not leave you orphaned" (14:18). All who believe in him are offered a family and a home.

Thus, at Cana and at the cross, we meet the bearer of divine gifts—extravagant gifts, beyond our imaginings—among them, the gift of a new family of faith, born in the moment when even his own life was laid down for his friends. Between those two points, further gifts will be offered, and thus we now follow the Word on the journey that unfolds between Cana and Calvary to grasp more of "his fullness," from which "we have all received, grace upon grace" (1:16).

POINTS OF COMPARISON

A quick glance at the other three Gospels may help us grasp the distinctive contribution that John makes to our understanding of Jesus, as important aspects of it emerge in John 2. Each evangelist performs functions similar to those performed by a newspaper editor, who must arrange a large number of stories at his or her disposal into a coherent whole. Decisions must be made about which stories make the front page and get the big headlines as the final layout is planned. Thus, as we read all of the Gospels, it is worth taking note of the story that each evangelist selects as the inaugural event of Jesus' public ministry, for that choice alerts us to characteristic aspects of their portraits of Jesus—emphases that are especially important to them. Of all the traditions at their disposal, which do they select as the most suitable introduction to Jesus' public ministry?

In the Gospel of Mark, the earliest of the Gospels, Jesus' public ministry is inaugurated with an exorcism (Mark 1:21–28). Jesus enters a synagogue in Capernaum on the Sabbath, where he finds himself in a loud and violent confrontation with a man possessed by an unclean spirit. It is an appropriate introduction to Mark's portrait of Jesus as one who throws himself into battle against the forces of evil, against all that distorts and disfigures human life. Indeed, the evangelist Mark includes a disproportionate number of "miracles" (or "acts of power") in his Gospel narrative, especially exorcisms, thereby highlighting the element of struggle in Jesus' ministry. The world is a place of bondage, in Mark's view, but through the words and actions of Jesus, God's agent, God's rule challenges every other claim to power.[10]

The Gospel of Matthew presents Jesus as the definitive teacher, who provides for his followers an authoritative interpretation of the will of God. Thus the "Sermon on the Mount" (Matt. 5–7), the first and foremost of five major teaching discourses in Matthew (Matt. 5–7, 10, 13, 18, 24–25), inaugurates Jesus' public ministry. Though long referred to as a "sermon," this extraordinary explication of life in the sphere of God's reign is actually "teaching" rather than "preaching," for we are told that when Jesus ascends the mountain, he "opened his mouth and taught them" (5:2), and when he comes down from the mountain at its conclusion, "the crowds were astonished at his teaching, for he taught them as one having authority" (7:28). Thus, technically speaking, it is a "Lecture on the Mount" rather than a sermon, and its inaugural role signals the special importance that Matthew attaches to Jesus' teaching ministry.

In the Gospel of Luke, Jesus' public ministry begins with an appearance on the Sabbath in his hometown synagogue (4:14–30), where he reads from the prophet Isaiah: "The Spirit of the Lord is upon me, because he has anointed me to bring good news to the poor. He has sent me to proclaim release to the captives and recovery of sight to the blind, to let the oppressed go free, to proclaim the year of the Lord's favor" (4:18–19). This serves Luke's interest in presenting Jesus as one whose life and ministry begins in the heart of Judaism and represents the fulfillment of God's promises to Israel, God's redemptive plan set forth in Scripture. Moreover, it presages Luke's portrait of Jesus as a liberator empowered by God's own Spirit, whose ministry will be marked by a deep concern for the poor and disenfranchised of the earth, for the oppressed and marginalized persons in society.

In like manner, the Gospel of John presents an inaugural scene appropriate to its own distinctive portrait of Jesus. At the wedding in Cana where Jesus provided vast quantities of wine, Jesus is presented as the giver of extravagant gifts to human beings—as one who came that we might "have life," and "have it abundantly" (10:10). Jesus' final miracle in John's Gospel, in its concluding chapter, is also a miracle of abundance: a miraculous catch of 153 fish (21:1–14). These miracles frame the Gospel on both ends, and we are given to understand that in this one, God's new age has arrived and God's abundant blessings are poured out on believers.

It is also worth noting that John's unique inaugural scene coheres with its unique introduction of Jesus as the cosmic Word, the agent of creation as well as of redemption, through whom all things came into being (1:1–4). At Cana, where his public ministry begins, the incarnate Word continues to exercise power over and within the created order; or, as a medieval commentator perceptively noted, "the water recognized its creator and blushed."[11]

QUESTIONS FOR DISCUSSION OR REFLECTION

Do a dramatic reading of John 2:1–12. Assign roles to a narrator, to Jesus, to his mother, and to a steward. Following the reading, share briefly: What intrigues or puzzles you most about the story of the wedding at Cana? What questions does it raise for you?

Interestingly, John does not narrate a story in which Jesus institutes the Lord's Supper (as do the other Gospels), and the question of whether the evangelist knew of this sacrament, or referred implicitly to it at any point, is hotly debated. Some find eucharistic symbolism implicit in the extravagant gift of wine at Cana, as well as in the extravagant gift of bread when five thousand are fed in John 6. What are your thoughts about this?

John's story of the wedding at Cana is often read today during Christian wedding ceremonies. Is this story an appropriate one for such occasions, in your view? What might it contribute to our understanding as we celebrate a wedding?

Gail O'Day points out that Jesus' first miracle in John takes place in the presence of friends and family, rather than in the presence of powers and authorities: "This opening to Jesus' ministry shows that the miraculous life-giving power of God is at work even (and perhaps, especially) in the intimate daily places of human lives."[12] Where have you most often found the abundant blessings of God in your life?

Had you noticed before the links between Cana and the cross? What do they contribute to your reflection on these stories? What do you make of Mary's role in both events?

What do you think of Beverly Gaventa's interpretation of Mary's role in John? Do you find it persuasive?

Examine the family imagery in 1:12–13; 3:3–10; 8:31–47; 14:1–3, 18–24; 16:20–24; 20:17; and discuss your reactions to it.

Do you experience your congregation as family? Do you think of fellow church members as siblings related to you by baptism and faith in Jesus Christ? Why, or why not?

Do those in your congregation who are not part of "nuclear families" as traditionally defined easily find a home in your church? What obstacles and opportunities come to mind as you think of the ways your congregation seeks to live out its faith as a family of God?

As you compare the inaugural events of Jesus' public ministry in Matthew, Mark, Luke, and John, what strikes you most? Which inaugural event appeals to you most, and why?

3

A Clandestine Encounter: Jesus and Nicodemus

John 3:1–21

Perhaps we may be forgiven if we find ourselves approaching John 3 with misgivings, for it is arguably the most sloganized, billboarded, bumper-stickered chapter in the New Testament. It provides the rallying cry of "born again" Christianity, as well as the New Testament's most frequently quoted verse: John 3:16. Those who have not heard John 3:16 in church have, no doubt, encountered it on *Monday Night Football*. It also introduces one of the New Testament's most ambiguous characters: Nicodemus, who finds himself in the midst of an utterly baffling conversation with Jesus—one that is guaranteed to baffle us as well.

A BAFFLING CONVERSATION ABOUT NEW BIRTH (3:1–10)

It is hard to know what to make of Nicodemus, one of the most intriguing yet elusive of biblical characters, for we are given decidedly mixed signals about him.[1] On the one hand, this seemingly sincere, learned Jewish leader takes the initiative to seek Jesus out and greets him with generous words of recognition: "Rabbi, we know that you are a teacher who has come from God; for no one can do these signs that you do apart from the presence of God" (3:2). On the other hand, one senses that Nicodemus's perception is limited, for Jesus is far more than a distinguished rabbi, a teacher approved by God: he is the Word made flesh, God's only Son, the very revelation of God (1:1–18). Moreover, Nicodemus is drawn to Jesus on the basis of the signs that he was doing, which places him among those to whom Jesus "did not entrust himself" in the immediately preceding verses (2:23–25). And although Nicodemus is a public figure—indeed, one who speaks confidently on behalf of his whole community ("we know . . .")—he does not approach Jesus publicly, but rather clandestinely, "by night," under cover of darkness (3:1).

It is also hard not to feel a measure of sympathy for, even empathy with, Nicodemus, for we may find ourselves every bit as befuddled as he is by Jesus' enigmatic conversation. Jesus has been described as one who "seems congenitally incapable of giving a straight answer"[2] in the Gospel of John, nowhere more so than in chapter 3 in his encounter with Nicodemus. Indeed, he neither acknowledges nor corrects Nicodemus's generous affirmation of God's presence in his ministry, responding instead with a puzzling teaching: "Very truly, I tell you, no one can see the kingdom of God without being born anew/born from above" (3:3).

Chapter 3 is the only place in John where reference to the "kingdom" or reign of God, so frequent in the other Gospels, appears; and Nicodemus experiences difficulty in comprehending what it means to be "born anew/born from above" and thus to see it—as might we all. Part of the difficulty is that the Greek word *anōthen* conveys two different meanings simultaneously: "born anew" and "born from above." It is impossible to capture both the temporal ("born anew") and spatial ("born from above") dimensions of *anōthen* with any single word in the English language, and thus English translations tend to choose one or the other of these meanings, thereby flattening it, as does Nicodemus. Stuck on the temporal dimension, he wonders how on earth it could be possible to be "born again." Frederick Buechner imagines his incredulity: "just how were you supposed to pull a thing like that off? How especially were you supposed to pull it off if you were pushing sixty-five? How did you get born again when it was a challenge just to get out of bed in the morning? He even got a little sarcastic. Could one 'enter a second time into the mother's womb?' he asked (John 3:4), when it was all one could do to enter a taxi without the driver's coming around to give him a shove from behind?"[3]

Another part of the problem is that Nicodemus's imagination (and perhaps ours as well) appears limited by preconceived understandings of what is possible and what is not. He is, after all, a respected religious leader and learned theologian, well schooled in religious matters. Indeed, his discourse is filled with statements about what is and is not possible with respect to things of God. Thus a literal translation of his initial greeting conveys his confident assertion that "*it is not possible* for one to do these signs apart from the presence of God." Now he inquires (literally), "*How is it possible* for anyone to be born after having grown old? *Surely it is not possible* to enter again into the mother's womb and be born?"

Moreover, Nicodemus undoubtedly knew himself to be a child of the covenant, part of God's chosen people, through birth from a Jewish mother, which may also account for his inability to comprehend the need to be "born again" to see the kingdom of God. However, the notion of a radical new birth should not be new to the reader of John's Gospel, for the prologue declared it to be the very purpose of the Word's incarnation: "to all who received him, who believed in his name, he gave power *to become children of God*, who *were born*, not of blood or of the will of the flesh or of the will of man, but of God" (1:12–13). This radical new birth is clearly God's doing, a regeneration accomplished by divine power alone. In short, it is "from above," which is why the spatial as well as the temporal dimension of *anōthen* is crucial.

Aiming to broaden the horizons of Nicodemus's vision, Jesus presses further, elaborating on what it means to be "born anew/born from above" and thus to see and enter the kingdom of God: it is to be "born of water and Spirit" (3:5). But Nicodemus can, perhaps, be forgiven for further befuddlement on his part, for commentators to this day continue to debate what, exactly, it means to be born of water and Spirit. In particular, to what does the "water" refer? Some have thought that the reference is to the human experience of birth, for the breaking of a mother's birth waters signals the imminent arrival of a child. Thus the reference would be to the necessity of both a physical birth and a spiritual birth, and Nicodemus would be given to understand that his own categories of birth are too limited. Perhaps he is also given to understand that human birth as a child of the covenant between God and Israel is, by itself, insufficient for entry into the kingdom of God, for "what is born of the flesh is flesh, and what is born of the Spirit is spirit" (3:6). Others, however, have thought that "water and Spirit" refer to one and the same thing: "water, that is, the Spirit," for water in the Fourth Gospel can be a symbol of the Spirit (see 7:38–39). Or perhaps Old Testament background music illumines Jesus' enigmatic metaphor, for in the Old Testament the washing of people in water and the outpouring of the Spirit will usher in the new age (Ezek. 36:25–27; Isa. 44:3). Nicodemus may thus be challenged to recognize the arrival of new life in the new age in the person of Jesus.[4] Yet another possibility presents itself: the reference to water has often been taken as a reference to Christian baptism and the new birth it signifies. Baptism is, after all, a central theme later in this chapter (see John 3:22, 26; 4:1), and was seen by the early church as a concrete sign of the Spirit's work and of Jesus' promise of new life and identity. Nicodemus may thereby be challenged to submit to Christian baptism, declaring public allegiance to a new community of faith.

Whatever the case may be, Jesus affirms the mystery and reality of which he speaks with yet another metaphor: that of the wind, which "blows where it chooses, and you hear the sound of it, but you do not know where it comes from or where it goes. So it is with everyone who is born of the Spirit" (3:8). The Greek word *pneuma* means both "wind" and "Spirit," and is thus a wordplay well suited to convey the unpredictability of the Spirit's movement. We can hear the sound of it and observe evidence of its presence, but we cannot predict, contain, or control its comings and goings. We may even find it inconvenient to open the window and let the breeze in, particularly, as commentator Tom Wright has noted, if we "have got things tidied up, labelled and sorted into neat piles."[5]

This may be part of Nicodemus's dilemma, for his final perplexed words reveal his inability in the end to relinquish his certitudes: "How can these things be possible?" (v. 9). Jesus notes the irony of the moment, a bit acerbically (3:10): the "teacher of Israel," who seemed to know all about Jesus at the beginning of the conversation, has demonstrated that he has no clue as to what Jesus is talking about. We may find ourselves in the very same position. Are we any clearer than Nicodemus as to what it means to be born anew/from above, to be born of water and Spirit, and thus to see and enter the kingdom of God?

MONOLOGICAL CLUES (3:11–21)

Nicodemus fades completely from view at this point, but if we stick around as dialogue shifts to monologue, Jesus may provide final important clues. First, he identifies himself clearly as "the one and only person in the human story who can lay claim to unveiling the mystery of God":[6] "No one has ascended into heaven except the one who descended from heaven, the Son of Man" (3:13). These words convey the distinctive vertical movement at the heart of John's Gospel, recalling the "descent" or incarnation of the eternal Word and anticipating his "ascent" or return to God. It is a restatement of the Fourth Gospel's central claim: Jesus is the fleshed-out truth about God (1:14, 18).

Second, Jesus, in allusive fashion, directs our attention to the cross, the moment of ascent in John in which he is "lifted up" from the earth (3:14; 8:28; 12:32–34)—a moment of "exaltation" in which he departs from the world and returns to God and the glory that was his before creation (the Greek word *hypsoō* means both "to lift up" and "to exalt" and represents yet another wordplay). The allusion is to an ancient story told in Numbers 21. When the rebellious Israelites were afflicted in their wilderness wanderings by poisonous snakes, God directed Moses to lift up a bronze serpent on a pole, so that anyone bitten by a snake might look upon it and live. In some mysterious way, Jesus' "lifting up" will also be a manifestation of the healing power of God, a moment when new life is available. Abstruse though it may be, it is the first of three passion predictions in John (3:14; 8:28; 12:32–34). Thus we are given to understand that somehow Jesus' "lifting up" on the cross is at the heart of what it means to be "born anew/born from above."

Indeed, later we will learn that the Spirit is given only after Jesus' "lifting up," his "glorification" on the cross (7:37–39; 20:22). Then the Spirit, "rivers of living water," shall flow "out of the believer's heart" (7:38–39). The cross, moreover, is a sign of the depth of God's love for the world (3:16), the extent to which that love is willing to go. "No one has greater love than this" (15:13). To John's way of thinking, the power of that love is utterly compelling, drawing us to Christ like a magnet (12:32) and overcoming our alienation from God. Therein lies the possibility of new birth and new life: in the cross that brings us face-to-face with the fullness of the life-giving love of God in Christ, and the rivers of living water that flow from it. Recognition of that love, revealed in Jesus' cross, accompanied by the gift of the Spirit, marks such a genuinely new beginning in our lives that it can only be spoken of as being "born again" or "anew." Therein lies "power to become children of God" (1:12).

But clearly there is nothing Nicodemus or any of us can do to secure the new birth of which Jesus speaks. Only divine initiative ("from above") can effect it, an initiative that springs from the immense love God has for the world (3:16). That love, however, is not coercive. The gift of it, visible in Jesus' cross and glorification, can either be received and embraced or rejected, and therein lies the reality of "judgment" in

John, a central theme that finds its clearest expression in the words that bring Jesus' discourse to a close (3:17–21).

These closing verses convey the Fourth Gospel's distinctive understanding of judgment, which is not explicitly associated with the end of history and the second coming of the Son of Man, as it is in Matthew, Mark, and Luke. John never denies a second coming, but focuses on the first, all-important coming down of Jesus from heaven before his public career, in the incarnation. As the Word made flesh, Jesus is the very revelation of God, the one who makes God known (1:14, 18). What this means is that whoever sees Jesus has already seen God (14:8–11), and thus judgment takes place right now in the attitude of faith or repudiation one assumes toward Jesus. Note: God and Jesus do not judge; self-judgment is in view. To John's way of thinking, we judge ourselves by our response to God's love in Jesus Christ. Those who receive it receive new life; but those who reject it cut themselves off from "eternal life," that is, from the rich quality or "fullness" of life that comes from living, both in the present and beyond death, in the unending presence of God (1:18; 10:10).[7]

While John 3 began with talk of new birth, Jesus concludes with talk of the quality of life: "And this is the judgment, that the light has come into the world, and people loved darkness rather than light because their deeds were evil. For all who do evil hate the light and do not come to the light, so that their deeds may not be exposed. But those who do what is true come to the light, so that it may be clearly seen that their deeds have been done in God" (3:19–21). The chapter also began with one who came to Jesus "by night" and then faded from view. But Nicodemus will make two further cameo appearances in John (7:45–52; 19:38–42). Will his deeds on those occasions demonstrate that he has finally come to the light?

CONNECTIONS

This story, like every story in the Gospel of John, seeks to bring us into an encounter with Jesus. What, then, can we learn from Nicodemus's encounter with him that can inform our own? A number of connections may be considered. First, Nicodemus is a character who may well evoke our sympathy, even empathy, as we too struggle to comprehend an enigmatic Jesus. He serves as a reminder that many people attracted to Jesus, then and now, do not immediately understand him.[8] Moreover, as no one of us fully understands Jesus until at the end when we shall be like him and see God as God is (1 John 3:2), all of us bear some resemblance to Nicodemus.[9]

However, religious people may find a special kinship with him. Nicodemus is a respected, educated theologian, well schooled in religious matters, and part of his problem may be that his imagination is limited by his certitudes about what is and is not possible with respect to things of God. Apparently, what we "know" can confine us and prevent us from embracing the mysterious life of the Spirit and God's own possibilities. Commentator Sandra Schneiders states the connection pointedly: "We are meant to identify with Nicodemus, thus recognizing ourselves as believers and at the same time mistrusting ourselves as those who too readily presume that they understand the Christian mystery. We, like Nicodemus, are religious people who tend to be overly confident in our faith-based religious knowledge. Like Nicodemus, we tend to be enslaved by the theological assumptions of the religious establishment so that we are not prepared to hear what is really new in the revelation of Jesus."[10]

Indeed, as a startling case in point, Schneiders notes that Christians have, for centuries, read John 3 "without realizing that the Fourth Evangelist here supplies us, through the voice of Jesus, with one of the clearest New Testament images of the femininity of God."[11] In his conversation with Nicodemus, Jesus employs the metaphor of coming forth from the mother's womb to describe new birth in the Spirit—a mystery too deep to be rendered by a single metaphor. However, "the biblical presentation of God as feminine has been virtually suppressed by the male religious establishment, which finds it as difficult to accept God in feminine imagery as the Jewish establishment found it to accept God in human form."[12] Could it be, as Schneiders suggests, that "accepting this revelation will revolutionize our God-experience as radically as the acceptance of Jesus' divinity revolutionized the God-experience of the Jews in John's community"?[13] Whatever the case may be, "Nicodemus is not a figure of the past. He lives in the heart of every believer who is tempted to settle down in the secure religious 'wisdom' of the establishment and thus resist the challenge of ongoing revelation."[14]

A second connection to ponder emerges when we take note of a peculiarity of the conversation in John 3: though it features two men speaking alone at night, they both employ plural forms of speech. Nicodemus, for example, greets Jesus saying "*We* know that you are a teacher who has come from God," and Jesus too employs "we" as well as plural forms of "you" (obscured in English translation): "*We* speak of what *we* know and testify to what *we* have seen; yet *you people* do not receive *our* testimony" (3:11; also 3:7, 12). What this suggests is that both Nicodemus and Jesus may speak as representative figures, reflecting a larger conversation of importance to the believers in John's early Christian community. Those Christians suffered expulsion from the synagogue for their forthright confession of faith in Jesus (an experience explicitly mentioned in 9:22; 12:42; 16:2). However, not all Jewish believers confessed Jesus publicly. Some remained in the synagogue as closet believers, or crypto-Christians, for fear of losing their position. The Gospel of John judges them harshly: "many, even of the authorities, believed in him. But because of the Pharisees they did not confess it, for fear that they would be put out of the synagogue; for they loved human glory more than the glory that comes from God" (12:42–43).

Nicodemus, who comes to Jesus "by night," under cover of darkness, may well represent these secret believers or closet Christians, and from this perspective Jesus' response to him may bear significant social implications. Commentator David Rensberger has made a compelling case for this, arguing that secret Christians like Nicodemus are challenged to come out of the closet and to submit to Christian baptism by Jesus' words in 3:5: "no one can enter the kingdom of God without being born of water and Spirit." The referent of "water" in 3:5 is much debated, but Rensberger makes a compelling case for it as a baptismal reference, for the theme of baptism is firmly anchored in the context of John 3 (see 3:22–26; 4:1–2). And baptism is not something one does in a closet. As Rensberger notes, it is a "public and social transaction" that openly acknowledges adherence both to Jesus as divine Son of God and to the community in which he is confessed.[15] In John's social environment, adherence to this community bore a cost: expulsion from the synagogue, dangerous social dislocation. Indeed, Nicodemus is being challenged to cross a social boundary and "to undertake an act of deliberate downward mobility":[16] "The choice that faced Nicodemus was whether or not to side, no longer in private but openly, with a specific oppressed group in his society—indeed, with those whom the members of his own rank and class, the people whose company he truly preferred, were oppressing."[17]

Rensberger's reading provides an important corrective to the individualistic piety so often associated with "born-again" Christianity, reminding us that the new birth of which Jesus speaks bears significant public, communal, and political implications. The implications continue to be challenging to ponder. Indeed, "Where is Nicodemus to be found today?" Rensberger answers pointedly:

> Nicodemus is to be found . . . where Christians in power relate to powerless Christians. This is true whether power is derived from money, class, gender, race, education, political connection, or otherwise. It applies to white Christians in relation to blacks in the United States and in South Africa. It applies to affluent members of church hierarchies in relation to peasants and the poor, in Latin America but certainly not only there. It applies to men in relation to women in nearly all societies. It applies to the educated in relation to the ignorant, the well fed in relation to the hungry, the healthy in relation to the sick. . . . Certainly it applies to any Christian who has not let this identity be known in a place where real danger might result. This includes those who are reluctant to become known as activists in struggles for justice and for peace, since . . . for John the one way in which Christians are known is by their love for one another.[18]

In short, "Nicodemus is to be found wherever one whose life is secure must face those whose life is insecure, or who struggle in the cause of God, and decide to say, 'I am one of them.'"[19]

Cannot both points of connection noted—the hazard of much too ready presumption that we understand the Christian mystery, and the social implications of new birth "by water and Spirit"—broaden our understanding of what it means to be "born anew/from above," and help us, perhaps, to reclaim it? The pervasive public rhetoric of "born again" piety often obscures these significant dimensions of John 3. Moreover, when *anōthen* is reduced to the temporal level ("born again" or "anew") and defined as a particular kind of religious conversion experience, its crucial spatial and christological dimensions ("born from above") are obscured as well. Indeed, Gail R. O'Day has perceptively noted: "Contemporary usage of 'born again' privileges anthropology over christology. That is, it emphasizes personal change more than the external source of that change: the cross. In Jesus' words in chap. 3, anthropology and christology are held in a delicate balance. That is, one cannot know the meaning of human life without grounding it in the reality of Jesus' life and the corporate dimension of that life. The irony of Nicodemus's response to Jesus' words is unwittingly operative whenever the church operates out of a single-level interpretation of *anōthen*."[20]

But John 3 is not the last word on Nicodemus, and so perhaps there is hope that both he and we can enter ever more deeply into the mysterious movements of the Spirit and the possibilities of God. Nicodemus, after all, makes two further appearances in John's Gospel, in chapters 7 and 19, and we are given mixed signals about him until the end.

In 7:45–52, when a manhunt is under way, Nicodemus reappears to defend Jesus before his fellow Pharisees, insisting that Jesus be accorded due process under the law. However, some see this as a timid legal squabble that falls short of open profession of faith. But Nicodemus reappears again after the death of Jesus (19:38–42) in the ambivalent company of Joseph of Arimathea (who is explicitly identified as a "secret" disciple of Jesus "because of his fear of the Jews"). Together, they wrap and bury the body of Jesus in a new garden tomb. Nicodemus's distinctive contribution to the burial is his provision of a "mixture of myrrh and aloes, weighing about a hundred pounds" (19:39). Some see this final gesture as a ludicrous and far too belated one, a sign of inadequate courage and faith to the end: "Nicodemus shows himself capable only of burying Jesus, ponderously and with a kind of absurd finality, so loading him down with burial as to make it clear that Nicodemus does not expect a resurrection any more than he expects a second birth."[21] But others argue that the gesture makes up for his earlier hesitancy. Though identified as one "who had at first come to Jesus by night" (19:39), he now appears before sunset (19:42) to perform a public act of true devotion, honoring Jesus with a burial befitting a king. Could it be that with these final appearances he aligns himself publicly with Jesus, showing himself to be among "those who do what is true" and "come to the light, so that it may be clearly seen that their deeds have been done in God" (3:21)? Perhaps the presence of these two secret disciples could also be said to represent the fulfillment of Jesus' own promise in 12:32: "I, when I am lifted up from the earth, will draw all people to myself." If so, their presence may be one final reminder that "faith is a human impossibility, but it can be engendered by the power of God." Indeed, "Joseph and Nicodemus may be the first indication of what Jesus' death would accomplish"[22]—a sign that "grace and newness of life are available even to those who try to say no."[23] For all who struggle to faith, this would be very good news indeed.

QUESTIONS FOR DISCUSSION OR REFLECTION

Do a dramatic reading of John 3:1–21. Assign roles to a narrator, to Jesus, and to Nicodemus. Following the reading, share briefly:

What most captures your attention as you hear the story? What questions does it raise for you?

Share your experience with and reactions to the phrase "born anew/born from above" (*anōthen*). What new insights did you gain about this phrase and how do they reframe your engagement with it?

Do you identify with Nicodemus? If so, how and why? If not, why not? What do you learn from Nicodemus's encounter with Jesus that can inform your own encounter with him?

What do you think of Schneiders's contention that we are meant to identify with Nicodemus, as believers who too readily presume we understand the Christian mystery and may resist the challenge of ongoing revelation?

Share your reaction to the feminine imagery for God employed in John 3. Had you ever noticed this before?

To what do you think the much-debated phrase "born of water and Spirit" (3:5) refers?

Share your experience with John 3:16. When did you first hear it? What does this well-known verse mean to you?

What do you think of John's distinctive understanding of judgment as a present reality and as self-judgment?

Share your reaction to Rensberger's contention that "Nicodemus is to found . . . where Christians in power relate to powerless Christians." Have you ever found yourself afraid to make your faith public, assuming the role of a closet disciple? In what contexts do you find public identification with Jesus and the Christian community most challenging?

How do you understand your own baptism? Does it include public, communal, political dimensions? How so?

Examine the subsequent appearances of Nicodemus in 7:45–52 and 19:38–42. What do you think they tell us about Nicodemus? Do you think he grows in faith, crossing the threshold of discipleship and aligning himself publicly with Jesus in the end? Why, or why not?

What new insights have emerged from your engagement with this story? What questions linger?

4

Conversation at the Well:
Jesus and the Woman of Samaria

John 4:1–42

John's portrait of the Samaritan woman who encounters Jesus at a well deserves special attention for at least two reasons. For one thing, her conversation with Jesus is the longest recorded conversation that he had with anyone. This fact is noteworthy in itself, but is especially so in John's Gospel, where Jesus is given to extensive monologues. (Wordy is the Lamb!) Few others get a word in edgewise. The Samaritan woman, however, finds herself engaged with Jesus in a genuine and extended conversation in which she holds her own quite well.

For another thing, her portrait has been clouded by considerable interpretive litter. The details of her marital history (narrated briefly in 4:16–18) have proved overly fascinating for generations of preachers and teachers, evoking imaginative (and often prurient) speculation about her circumstances and character. As Fred Craddock observes: "Evangelists aplenty have assumed that the brighter her nails, the darker her mascara and the shorter her skirt, the greater the testimony to the power of the converting word."[1] Sandra Schneiders states the case more bluntly: "The treatment of the Samaritan woman in the history of interpretation is a textbook case of the trivialization, marginalization and even sexual demonization of biblical women."[2] Consequently, much has been read into her portrait, while notable features of it unrelated to her sexual history have, sadly, been overlooked. Attend closely then to the way that John describes her, and to her remarkable encounter with Jesus, in hopes of recovering a more accurate portrait.

CONTEXTUAL CONSIDERATIONS

Several contextual issues (historical and literary) are noteworthy as we begin to examine this portrait. In terms of historical context, John 4 departs from what we know of Jesus' ministry in the other Gospels, for only John mentions a ministry of Jesus in Samaria. Because this is not corroborated anywhere else in the New Testament, that the historical Jesus carried out a mission in Samaria is perhaps unlikely. This scene probably represents the experience of Johannine Christians who embraced Samaritan converts as brothers and sisters in Christ. Therefore, as we read the story, we should keep in mind that the woman Jesus encounters at the well has a symbolic function: she represents the Samaritan presence within the Johannine Christian community. Indeed, as she appears on the scene in verses 7–9, she is described three times as a "Samaritan woman." She is not given a name. Instead, her national identity is underlined. Moreover, in the course of her extended conversation with Jesus, she raises a variety of religious and theological issues that were key matters of dispute between Jews and Samaritans (see vv. 9, 12, 20). She functions in the story as a spokesperson for the Samaritan people.

For additional historical context, we should note that first-century Jews and Samaritans had been divided by centuries of hostility and deep prejudice. They shared a common heritage, each maintaining they were the bearers of the true faith of ancient Israel. They differed radically, however, in regard to the relative sanctity of Jerusalem and Mount Gerizim (see 4:20), and also held different legal and scriptural traditions. Samaritans were considered heretics, foreigners, and unclean by Jews, who avoided contact with them (see 4:9). However, Jesus is presented as deliberately crossing this ethnic and religious boundary. Indeed, as the story opens, the narrator whispers to us that "he had to go through Samaria" (4:4; or translating more literally, "it was necessary" for him to pass through Samaria). Though the main route from Judea to Galilee was through Samaria, Jesus could easily have avoided it; many Jews did. The narrator thus speaks not of geographical necessity, but of theological necessity—the divine imperative of Jesus' presence among the Samaritan people.[3]

In terms of literary context, the woman Jesus encounters in chapter 4 is the mirror opposite of the individual he engages in chapter 3 (Nicodemus), and a clear contrast is established between the two. Indeed, they are at opposite ends of the social, political, and religious spectrum.[4] One is a named male; the other is an unnamed female. One is a distinguished religious leader, a pillar of the community; the other is a despised foreigner with an irregular marital history. Other contrasts emerge: Nicodemus comes to Jesus by night, whereas the Samaritan woman encounters Jesus at noon, in the fullest light of day. The dialogue between Jesus and Nicodemus quickly shifts into one of Jesus' monologues, and Nicodemus fades into the shadows. We have no idea how he responds to Jesus or if he responds at all, for his subsequent appearances in 7:50–51 and 19:39 are ambiguous in nature.[5] The conversation between Jesus and the Samaritan woman, by contrast, is characterized by lively give-and-take. Indeed, it is "one of the few occasions in this Gospel in which a dialogue between Jesus and another character does not become a monologue for Jesus alone."[6] Moreover, at the conclusion of her story, the Samaritan woman does something very important that Nicodemus did not do: she bears witness to Jesus. As a result, a whole village comes to faith.

Finally, an Old Testament literary connection is significant, for in John 4 we hear echoes of an old familiar story: boy meets girl at a well. It is how Isaac met Rebekah, Jacob met Rachel, and Moses met Zipporah (Gen. 24; 29; Exod. 2). The recognized biblical pattern (called a "betrothal type-scene") unfolds, more or less, in this manner: the future bridegroom journeys to a foreign land, where he encounters a girl at a well, and one of them draws water. Afterward, the girl rushes to bring home the news of the stranger's arrival. Finally, a betrothal is concluded between the stranger and the girl, after he has been invited to a meal.[7]

John follows this pattern, but with a few wrinkles. Jesus travels to a foreign country, and like his biblical predecessors meets a woman at a well. Like Jacob, he meets her there in broad daylight, at noon. However, Jesus meets not a maiden but a five-time married woman. And rather than looking for a wife, he is looking for worshipers in spirit and truth. The woman does rush home to share the news, but there is no betrothal meal. Rather, Jesus declares that his food is to do the will of the one who sent him and complete God's work. However, he does visit her home and accepts the hospitality extended to him by the Samaritan community, staying two days. There is joy all around, though the story ends not with betrothal but with the conversion of the whole Samaritan community to faith in Jesus as "Savior of the world" (4:42).

The echoes deepen when we take note of the marital motif that runs throughout John 2–4: Jesus' public ministry begins, in John 2, with a wedding at Cana, and in 3:29 he is pointedly referred to as "the bridegroom." On the heels of this, a boy meets a girl at a well in John 4. What is one to make of this narrative?

As strange as it seems, the scene in John 4 has been interpreted as an attempted seduction on the part of the woman. Lyle Eslinger discerns sexual innuendos throughout the conversation, noting the sexual orientation of the imagery of living water, springs, wells, and cisterns in the Old Testament, for example. Proverbs 5:15–18: "Drink water from your own cistern, flowing water from your own well . . . and rejoice in the wife of your youth."[8] I cannot endorse Eslinger's reading, but it does illustrate what can happen if one completely sexualizes the scene and runs wild with this line of interpretation. Sandra Schneiders has suggested a fascinating alternative and plausible interpretation: she calls attention to the use of marital imagery in Israel's prophetic literature to describe the relationship between Yahweh and the covenant people. In this scene, Jesus, "the new Bridegroom who assumes the role of Yahweh, bridegroom of ancient Israel, comes to claim Samaria as an integral part of the New Israel, namely, the Christian community."[9]

Another Old Testament connection sheds further light on the story in this regard, for the woman's personal history parallels the Samaritan national history as detailed in 2 Kings 17:24ff. In that account, we learn that when the Assyrians conquered the region in 721 BC, they brought colonists from five foreign nations into Samaria. Thus the woman's five previous husbands may well be symbolic of Samaria's intermarriage with foreign peoples and the acceptance of their false gods. And what about the sixth man? Perhaps the current man is Rome, for colonization continued under first-century Roman rule. The Jewish historian Josephus tells us that the Samaritans lived together with the foreigners, but did not intermarry with the Roman colonists as extensively as under the Assyrians.[10] Alternatively, cohabitation with a sixth man might refer to the Samaritans' syncretistic worship of Yahweh in the New Testament era, worship that lacked the full integrity of the covenant relationship.[11] Whichever the case may be, the woman's personal history of marriage to five husbands and cohabitation with a sixth may well symbolize the colonial history of Samaria.[12] Indeed, Schneiders suggests that "the entire dialogue between Jesus and the woman is the 'wooing' of Samaria to full covenant fidelity in the New Israel by Jesus, the New Bridegroom."[13]

THE POINT OF THE CONVERSATION

The Samaritan woman's marital history has more often been interpreted along rather different lines, with imaginative results. Indeed, much has been made of her sinfulness, her shady past, her dubious morals, her promiscuity, her aberrant sexual behavior. John Calvin serves as an instructive example. He imagined that she must have been a difficult and disobedient wife, who thereby "constrained her husbands to divorce her." "Though God joined thee to lawful husbands, thou didst not cease to sin, until, rendered infamous by numerous divorces, thou prostitutedst thyself to fornication." Moreover, Calvin speculates that "Christ, in order to repress the woman's talkativeness, brought forward her former and present life."[14] No comment!

Let us be clear about this fact: the text tells us that the Samaritan woman had five husbands, but it does not tell us why. We do not know whether she has been divorced or widowed. Perhaps like Tamar in Genesis 38, she is trapped in the custom of levirate marriage, and the last male in the family line has refused to marry her.[15] Moreover, we should bear in mind that divorce (which is not mentioned in the text) was an exclusively male privilege. Could it be that her husbands found her lacking or unlovely, and rid themselves of responsibility and relationship, as husbands of that time were entitled to do?[16] Possibly. Is she guilty of sexual sin? Maybe—maybe not. We may discern that she has had a tragic personal history of some sort, but the details are not available to us. To focus single-mindedly on these issues may well miss the main point of the conversation. Gail O'Day makes an important observation in this regard:

> When we read vv. 16–19 carefully, we notice that the history of the woman's five husbands is presented quite disinterestedly, with no suggestion or coloring of moral outrage or judgment. How or why the woman has had five husbands and the quality of those marriages are not a concern of the Evangelist as he tells the story. More importantly, those questions are also unimportant to Jesus. One searches in vain for any words of judgment about the woman's character uttered by Jesus in these verses.[17]

O'Day insists that "the conversation of vv. 16–19 is intended to show the reader something about Jesus, not primarily about the woman."[18]

What do we learn about Jesus in the course of their conversation? A number of important things. For one, in the first round of their conversation (vv. 7–15) we learn that he crosses boundaries between male and female and between chosen and rejected people, demonstrating that the grace of God is available to all.[19] He makes that gift available to all as he offers the Samaritan woman living water, a symbol of the gift of God that he represents (3:16), and also of the new life or the Spirit that God gives to us in Christ (7:37–39).[20] People who drink of it will never be thirsty, for the gift of God fills our whole being and runs over, penetrating every part of human existence. Although the Samaritan woman does not fully grasp what he offers, she is open to Jesus and asks him to give her this water, as he has invited her to do.

In the second round of their conversation (vv. 16–26), Jesus continues to draw the Samaritan woman to faith with a reference to her marital history that illustrates his ability to see and know all things.[21] Stunned by Jesus' extraordinary knowledge of her life, the woman is now able to see him with new eyes: "I see that you are a prophet" (v. 19). This being the case, she sets before him what was at that time the most critical theological question separating Jews and Samaritans: Is God to be worshiped in Jerusalem as Jews maintained, or on the mountain of Gerizim as Samaritans believed (v. 20)? Unfortunately, many commentators do not see this as a serious theological query on her part, but as a smokescreen, a diversionary tactic, a desperate attempt to change the topic and extricate herself from an embarrassing conversation. Others cannot imagine that she would be capable of theological inquiry. (For example, one distinguished Johannine scholar says this in his otherwise magnificent commentary: "We may still wonder if a Samaritan woman would have been expected to understand even the most basic ideas of the discourse."[22])

She ought not to be devalued as a legitimate conversation partner. In the circumstances of that time, the question she asks is a risky, courageous, and deeply theological one. (And, if the Samaritan history of syncretistic worship is in view in 4:18 when five husbands are mentioned, then her question about true worship hardly represents a "shift" in the conversation, but rather a probing continuation of it.) In Jesus' answer, we learn that the Spirit he gives is not bound to any location, and enables believers to worship God properly, "in spirit and truth" (vv. 21–24). As their conversation concludes, he discloses that he is the expected Messiah and more, for the words "I am" ("I am he" in many translations; see 4:26) link his very being with that of the one revealed to Moses in the burning bush (Exod. 3:14). This is the first time these striking words appear in the Fourth Gospel, and the Samaritan woman is the first to hear them.

BEARING WITNESS

Older lectionaries amputated the Samaritan woman's story, concluding with verse 26. The Revised Common Lectionary is an improvement, encouraging us to continue through verse 42. Doing so is important, for three concluding scenes in verses 27–42 are integral to the story.

First, in a fascinating transitional scene (vv. 27–30), Jesus' disciples return and the Samaritan woman temporarily exits. On their return, the disciples are "astonished that he was speaking with a woman" (v. 27), though a more literal translation of the Greek (*ethaumazon*) suggests a continuing state of shock rather than mere "astonishment." Curiously, they are shocked not because he is talking with a Samaritan, but because he is talking with a woman. In marked contrast to the woman's straight-forward questioning of Jesus, they do not openly question and challenge Jesus' purposes in doing so (v. 27).

At this point, the woman leaves her water jar and returns to the city, saying to the people: "Come and see a man who told me everything I have ever done! He cannot be the Messiah, can he?" The abandoned water jar, an intriguing detail, teases our imaginations and is open to varied interpretations. Perhaps it conveys the woman's enthusiasm and haste to share her news; perhaps she has no further need for it as she is now in possession of living water and will never thirst again (4:14); maybe even she herself has become a vessel for the gospel. Alternatively, some see it as the Johannine feminine counterpart to the Synoptic presentation of male disciples leaving their nets and boats behind to follow Jesus,[23] or more simply, as an indication that the woman intends to return to the well. Her story is not finished yet.[24]

Whatever the case may be, we would also do well to attend to her words of witness before her compatriots. "Come and see a man who told me everything I have ever done!" (v. 29), as Fred Craddock observes, is "not exactly a recitation of the Apostles Creed."[25] We should also note the question mark in her voice: "He cannot be the Messiah, can he?" (v. 29). Her faith is tentative, not yet mature, but she is moved by the presence of Jesus and eager to share the news, wanting her friends to encounter him too. This response on her part is a critical dimension of her portrait, not to be overlooked. Here she embodies one of the primary marks of discipleship in John: bearing witness to Jesus. Moreover, it should not escape us that faith that is tentative, full of questions, and not yet mature, can bear witness and do so effectively.

Following the transitional scene in verses 27–30, a conversational interlude with the disciples in verses 31–38 addresses their skepticism and vindicates the Samaritan woman. The disciples are told to lift their eyes and see the fields already white for harvest as the Samaritans pour out of their city and make their way toward Jesus. The Samaritan woman has sown the seed, and they may now reap. She has labored, and they may enter into her labor. What the disciples learn is that mission is shared labor and responsibility that includes both women and men, a fact that may be hard for them to swallow. Indeed, Sandra Schneiders observes:

> The brief episode of the return of the disciples, viewed from a feminist perspective, reveals the all-too-familiar uneasiness of men when one of their number takes a woman too seriously, especially in the area of men's primary concern. Jesus' discourse about his mission and its extension into Samaria only serves to confirm their worst fears, that they are neither the originators nor the controllers of the church's mission. The effectiveness of the woman's evangelization of her town caps this scene, in which any male claim to a privileged or exclusive role in the work of Jesus is definitively undermined by Jesus' own words and deeds.[26]

Finally, the conclusion to the story in verses 39–42 underlines the effectiveness of the Samaritan woman's ministry: "Many Samaritans from that city believed in him because of the woman's testimony" (v. 39). She is a success in spite of herself, in spite of her own tentative faith. Though the story began with a notation that "Jews do not share things in common with Samaritans" (v. 9), it ends on a note of reversal, as the Samaritans invite Jesus to stay. As Jesus accepts their hospitality and remains (or "abides") with them two days, "many more believed because of his word. They said to the woman, 'It is no longer because of what you said that we believe, for we have heard for ourselves, and we know that this is truly the Savior of the world'" (vv. 41–42).

Some interpreters have viewed this closing comment as denigrating the woman and dismissing her role in bringing the Samaritans to faith. (Calvin, for example, notes: "The Samaritans appear to boast that they have now a stronger foundation than a woman's tongue, which is, for the most part, light and trivial."[27]) However, this is the pattern of faith development and discipleship in John. Faith has powerful results when it is shared with others; but faith based on the witness of others must move on to a firsthand experience of Jesus.[28] The Samaritan woman's missionary task is fulfilled when the Samaritans make this transition and their own confession of faith in Jesus as Savior of the world.

In sum, revisions of the Samaritan woman's portrait seem to be in order. In the history of interpretation, much has been made of her irregular marital history but very little of her witness, her missionary endeavor, or Jesus' vindication of her role against the disapproval of male disciples. She is much more than a woman with an interesting love life or a model of sin. She is the first character in John to engage Jesus in serious theological conversation. Moreover, she is the most effective evangelist in this whole Gospel, hence a model for Christian faith and witness. As Robert Kysar observes, "Because of her the reader of the Gospel knows that no matter who you are—no matter what your status in society may be—the revelation of God in Christ is for you!"[29]

QUESTIONS FOR DISCUSSION OR REFLECTION

Before beginning your study of John 4, share: What impressions of the Samaritan woman do you bring with you to your present study of her portrait? What comes to mind when you think of her, and why? How do you remember hearing her described?

Do a dramatic reading of John 4:4–42. Assign roles to a narrator, to Jesus, and to a Samaritan woman. Have the rest of the group read collectively the lines of both the disciples and the Samaritan townspeople. Following the reading, share briefly: What most captures your attention as you hear the story? What questions does the story raise for you?

How do the historical and literary contextual observations noted at the beginning of this chapter contribute to your reading of the story? Any new insights or surprises?

Are you inclined to take the reference to the woman's five husbands literally or symbolically? Why?

Much has been made of the fact that the woman appeared at the well at noon, the hottest hour of the day. How have you heard this fact interpreted? What do you make of it? When this story is conveyed in preaching or teaching, many say that the hour conveys the contempt in which the woman is held by others. She comes to the well at noon, when it is deserted, to avoid any public humiliation. However, (1) isn't "light" a central, positive image throughout the Gospel of John, from beginning to end? (2) Isn't the hour in which she appears one of the striking contrasts between the woman and Nicodemus? (Nicodemus comes to see Jesus by night, under the cover of darkness, whereas the Samaritan woman encounters Jesus at noon, in the fullest light of day.) (3) What of the echoes of the old familiar story: boy meets girl at a well? Do they not also caution us against imputing moral significance to the noon hour? Jesus meets the woman at the well at noon, just like Jacob, who met Rachel at a well at noon, in broad daylight. But do we ever say, "O Rachel, what a slut. She was there because no one wanted to have anything to do with her"? Do you run errands at times when places of business are likely to be more or less crowded? Is it possible that the Samaritan woman's workload might have required multiple trips to the well?[30] In sum, is this yet another point at which we are reading a lot of trash into the story?

Gossip, sexual innuendos, and tragic marital circumstances are often allowed to "define" people completely, clouding our perception of their gifts and achievements and dignity as children of God. Would you agree? Do other examples come to mind, in addition to that of the Samaritan woman?

Water is one of the central images in John. Throughout, there are conversations about water, water pots, rivers, wells, springs, the sea, pools, basins, thirst, and drink.[31] What is the significance of water in human life? What does this suggest about Jesus, who in John 4 uses living water as the symbol for the gift he represents and for the new life or the Spirit of which he is the giver and source?

In the first-century world, Jews and Samaritans were divided by centuries of hostility and deep prejudice. Though they shared a common heritage, Samaritans were considered heretics, foreigners, and unclean by Jews, who avoided contact with them (this history is reflected in John 4:9). Who are the "Samaritans" in our world? How might we follow Jesus' example and cross boundaries that separate us from such persons? Should we?

Verse 28 provides a fascinating detail: "the woman left her water jar" as she went back to the city. What do you make of this detail? In your view, what does it convey?

In what ways do you identify with the Samaritan woman?

How can the Samaritan woman's tentative witness inform your own discipleship? Who are the persons in your life who risked sharing their own faith stories, thereby drawing you into relationship with Jesus Christ?

What new insights have emerged for you from your engagement with this story? What questions remain?

5

Images of Life

John 6; 8–9; 10; 14; 15

A picture is worth a thousand words—or so it is said. Perhaps this is why some of the most memorable words in all of the Gospel of John are those in which Jesus employs vivid images or word pictures to illuminate both who he is and what he represents in the lives of believers: "I am the bread of life. . . . I am the light of the world. . . . I am the good shepherd. . . . I am the vine, you are the branches." Interestingly, Jesus does not suggest that he is "similar" to bread, or "sort of like" light, or to be "compared" to a vine. His claim is absolute: "I am *the* bread of life. . . . I am *the* light of the world. . . . I am *the* vine."

The images that Jesus employs often appear in conjunction with two words that are themselves rather dramatic: "I am" (in Greek, the emphatic construction *egō eimi*). Many among John's first audience would have felt the hair rise on the back of their necks on hearing those words, for "I AM" was the divine name revealed by God to Moses in the burning bush: "Moses said to God, 'If I come to the Israelites and say to them, "The God of your ancestors has sent me to you," and they ask me, "What is his name?" what shall I say to them?' God said to Moses, 'I AM WHO I AM.' He said further, 'Thus you shall say to the Israelites, "I AM has sent me to you"'" (Exod. 3:13–14; see also Deut. 32:39; Isa. 43:10, 25; 45:18; 51:12). The divine name was and is regarded by Jews as sacred, not to be uttered by human beings. Only God can speak this way—which is exactly John's point. Jesus can dare to speak the sacred

41

name because he is the Word made flesh who "makes God known" (1:18), the one in whom God's identity is revealed.

John's "I AM" sayings are thus among the highest claims for the divinity of Christ in the entire New Testament.[1] Sometimes the words "I AM" stand alone (as in 4:26 or 18:6; though translators often fill in a predicate, e.g., "I am he."). More often, they are used in conjunction with vivid images that illustrate the meaning of Jesus' relationship to us as the bread, the light, the door, the shepherd, the way, or the vine (6:35, 51; 8:12; 9:5; 10:7, 9, 11, 14; 11:25; 14:6; 15:1, 5). These striking images, our focus in this chapter, are drawn from the ordinary stuff of this earth, the fabric of daily life. Though Jesus comes "from above," he uses images "from below," from this world, to convey his message. He calls upon things that can be "heard, seen, touched, and tasted to bear witness to the unseen God who sent him."[2] Indeed, John's theology can be described as an extraordinarily sensory, even sacramental one: "The Ultimate Reality of the universe—God—is to be experienced through the mundane sensory experiences of life!"[3] This is as it should be, for the earth is God's creation, and Jesus is the very Word through which "all things came into being" (1:3). Let us turn our attention to these common images that Jesus employs to speak of his saving relationship to us and to all people.

"I AM THE BREAD OF LIFE" (6:35–59)

The first image that Jesus employs in "I AM" sayings is the image of bread, the very staff of life: "I am the bread of life. Whoever comes to me will never be hungry" (6:35). No image could convey more clearly Jesus' power to nourish and sustain human life and to address our ultimate hunger—the hunger in every human heart for relationship with God.

Jesus' use of the bread image would have evoked a range of associations among many who first heard it. Chief among these would have been the memories of the Israelites' wilderness wanderings, during which they were fed daily by manna, miraculous bread from heaven. Jesus himself performs another miraculous feeding at the beginning of John 6, the feeding of the five thousand (6:1–14), in the wake of which the crowd becomes so enthusiastic that they seek to make him king (6:14–15). However, Jesus recognizes that their real interest is in another free lunch (6:26). Thus he draws a clear distinction between "food that perishes" (like manna or the miraculous lunch) and "food that endures for eternal life," urging attention to the latter (6:27). Then, in the Bread of Life Discourse that follows (6:35–59), he boldly identifies himself as the very bread of life, come down from heaven, who sustains people in a relationship with God that lasts forever. Indeed, his death on the cross (the giving of his own "flesh") manifests the fullness of God's love, drawing humans into a lasting relationship with God that begins now in faith and endures beyond the grave: "I am the bread of life. Your ancestors ate the manna in the wilderness, and they died. This is the bread that comes down from heaven, so that one may eat of it and not die. I am the living bread that came down from heaven. Whoever eats of this bread will live forever; and the bread that I will give for the life of the world is my flesh" (6:48–51).

Two other associations echo throughout the Bread of Life Discourse. In the Jewish Scriptures, bread is also associated with God's word and God's wisdom (see Amos 8:11–13; Prov. 9:5; Isa. 55:10–11)—with revelation and teaching—and is thus an appropriate metaphor for the ultimate divine teacher, who reveals the truth about God and human life. Moreover, eucharistic implications abound (especially in John 6:52–58, where "eat," "feed," "drink," "flesh," and "blood" vocabulary is concentrated). The Lord's Supper is indeed a means by which we continue to receive a share in God's own life. But even those unfamiliar with the Scriptures or the sacraments know the importance of bread: where there is no bread, life cannot flourish. By identifying himself as "the bread of life" come down from heaven, Jesus claims to be the gift of God and the basis for all life.[4]

"I AM THE LIGHT OF THE WORLD" (8:12)

The second image Jesus employs in an "I AM" saying is that of light: "I am the light of the world. Whoever follows me will never walk in darkness but will have the light of life" (8:12). Striking imagery of light and darkness pervades the Fourth Gospel from its opening verses, where the Word made flesh is identified as the source of life that is "the light of all people"—a light that "shines in the darkness" that the darkness has not "overcome" (1:4–5). But in 8:12 Jesus embraces the image of light, stating unambiguously his singular role as revealer, as the one through whom God's light shines, and the one who illumines the meaning and purpose of human life.

Jesus' use of this image has important implications for discipleship as

well. Our response to the light of God manifest in Christ has implications for how we "walk," that is, for how we live in relationship with
him. Light can illumine our path and our walking. However, if we obstinately stare at it and refuse to recognize its power, we can be blinded.[5]
All of these dimensions of the image find powerful expression in one of
John's most dramatic stories: the healing of the man born blind (chap.
9), which we will examine in chapter 7 of this study.

"I AM THE DOOR OF THE SHEEP . . . I AM
THE GOOD SHEPHERD" (10:1–18)

In 10:1–18 our imagination is set spinning, for Jesus is represented as
drawing to himself varied images suggested by the picture of sheep and
shepherd. The "I AM" sayings clustered in this text invite the community of faith, God's beloved flock, to reflect upon its relationship to the
one who is the door to life and the shepherd of God's sheep.

Jesus describes himself as the "door" (RSV) or "gate" (NRSV) of
the sheep in verses 7–10: "Very truly, I tell you, I am the gate of the
sheep. . . . Whoever enters by me will be saved, and will come in and go
out and find pasture." The image of the "door" or "gate" may be less familiar to us as a biblical image of Jesus than that of "shepherd," but its focus
is clear: the single means of access to all that is good is Jesus. It is through
him that we gain entry into the beloved flock of God. Moreover, he is the
gate leading to salvation, for it is through him that we have access to the
pasture of life, the abundant fullness of life intended by the Creator.

The image of a "door" or "gate" may not be as appealing as that of a
shepherd. But we ought not to overlook its implications for the community of faith, particularly as we bear in mind that the Christians to
whom the Gospel of John was first addressed had been kicked out the
door of the synagogue for their confession of faith (9:22, 34; 12:42;
16:2). We stand far removed from the evangelist's historical context and
struggle with Judaism, and should avoid anti-Jewish interpretations of
the text in our own setting. Indeed, there is no need to point the finger
at Judaism, for Jesus' words invite our reflection on the nature of our
own communities of faith: are we closed-in communities, or open-door
communities, who receive and welcome all sorts and conditions of people into our fellowship, as did Jesus? Have we ever played the role of
hirelings and thieves by shutting church doors against those seeking the
abundant life and seeking to enter the sanctuary?[6] John 10 reminds us

that we are not the door—Jesus is! And "the door Jesus Christ always has the welcome mat out."[7]

The imagery spins in verses 11–18: "I am the good shepherd. The good shepherd lays down his life for the sheep. . . . I am the good shepherd. I know my own and my own know me." Here Jesus draws on familiar Old Testament imagery, for the figure of the shepherd had long been applied to the rulers of the people and used to describe God's special care for Israel (see Ps. 23; Ezek. 34). Indeed, one of the most arresting features of Jesus' discourse in John 10 is that he speaks of himself as the kind of shepherd that the Old Testament suggests only God can be. He mediates God's pastoral care to the sheep.

Two important dimensions of his pastoral care are highlighted. One is his radical commitment to the community of faith, demonstrated above all by his willingness to give his life for them: "I am the good shepherd. The good shepherd lays down his life for the sheep" (v. 11). He lays it down freely of his own accord: "No one takes it from me" (v.18). The other distinguishing dimension of Jesus' pastoral care is its intimacy: "I am the good shepherd, I know my own and my own know me, just as the Father knows me and I know the Father. And I lay down my life for the sheep" (vv. 14–15). The language of "knowing" in John is always the language of intimate relationship (rather than of intellectual understanding). The same intimacy of relationship that exists between Jesus and his Father embraces all who have been entrusted to the shepherd's care. Indeed, "He calls his own sheep by name . . . and the sheep follow him because they know his voice" (10:3–4).

The image of the good shepherd is one of the most endearing of all John's snapshots of Jesus, and perennially relevant. False shepherds abound in the world, competing for our attention—imposters who would claim the shepherd's mantle, promising security of various kinds. John reminds us that only one has demonstrated his love for us by dying for us, thereby gathering us into a beloved community where each is embraced as infinitely precious in God's sight.

"I AM THE WAY, AND THE TRUTH, AND THE LIFE" (14:6)

During his final meal with his disciples on the night before his death, as he bid them farewell, Jesus employed another striking image to convey the meaning of his relationship to them: that of "the way." It was offered as a powerful word of reassurance for his anguished followers, who were about to lose the one who was the center of their life together. He had just spoken of his Father's house and its many dwelling places, where he was going to prepare a place for them. "And you know the way to the place where I am going," he said, to which Thomas objected: "Lord, we do not know where you are going. How can we know the way?" Jesus assured them that they did indeed know the way, for they knew him: "I am the way, and the truth, and the life. No one comes to the Father except through me" (14:6).

It is a traveler's image, appropriate for the journey Jesus is about to complete.[8] He is on his way to being reunited with his Father in glory. God is the destination, and the route Jesus will follow is the way of the cross.[9] Moreover, he makes it possible for others, too, to be united with the Father. Thus, by identifying himself as "the way," Jesus assures disciples that they have access to the Father, a sure and clear way to God.

"Truth" and "life" stand in apposition to "the way," and thus they clarify how and why Jesus is the way. The reality of God is the absolute truth in John, and Jesus is the way for disciples because he is their point of access to that truth, revealing the love of God and the meaning of human existence in relation to its gracious Creator. And because he lives in the Father and the Father lives in him, he is the channel through which the Father's life comes to disciples—a rich quality of life that emerges from the transforming and fulfilling experience of intimate relationship with God and is fully accessible now through Jesus.

The words "I am the way, and the truth, and the life" continue to convey who Jesus is for us, expressing the joyous conviction that through Jesus, the incarnate Word, we have access to God. But in recent years, the second half of 14:6 has proved controversial: "No one comes to the Father except through me." These words have an exclusionary ring that many find deeply problematic and downright embarrassing in a religiously plural world; but others find in them an essential tenet, indeed, a litmus test, of authentic Christian faith. Thus they have become fighting words among believers. As the debate is often framed, is Jesus "the only way of salvation," or not? Do his words condemn people of any and all other religious faiths?

As Gail O'Day wisely observes, however, 14:6 is problematic when it is used to speak to questions that were never within the Gospel's purview:

> To use these verses [14:6–7] in a battle over the relative merits of the world's religions is to distort their theological heart. . . . The

Fourth Gospel is not concerned with the fate, for example, of Muslims, Hindus, or Buddhists, nor with the superiority or inferiority of Judaism and Christianity as they are configured in the modern world. These verses are the confessional celebration of a particular faith community, convinced of the truth and life it has received in the incarnation. The Fourth Evangelist's primary concern was the clarification and celebration of what it means to believe in Jesus (14:1, 10–11).[10]

Indeed, 14:6 expresses a core claim of Christian identity: "This is who we are. We are the people who believe in the God who has been revealed to us decisively in Jesus Christ,"[11] and shaped by this identity we take our place in conversations about world religions.[12]

As we engage those conversations, we do well to keep the context of 14:6 in mind. In its literary context, 14:6 is addressed to insiders, offering comfort and assurance to fragile disciples in distress rather than a weapon with which to bludgeon others. Historical context is equally important, for the exclusionary ring of 14:6b reflects the pain of a small sect struggling for its existence after exclusion from the synagogue. Indeed, as David Rensberger notes,

> When these statements were written, their author was in no position to oppress or coerce anyone on the basis of them. Christianity was a powerless entity only beginning to appear on the crowded stage of Hellenistic-Roman religion. . . . Such claims to exclusive possession of the truth are not uncommon among sectarian movements. . . . It is not the arrogance of a world religion claiming all truth for itself in competition with other groups of comparable antiquity and influence. It is the defiance of a sect that has suffered exclusion itself and now hurls exclusion back in the teeth of its oppressors.[13]

It is also worth noting that Jesus does *not* say, "No one comes to *God* except through me," but rather that "No one comes to the *Father* except through me." Christians do believe that an encounter with Jesus Christ, God's Son, makes possible a new experience of God as Father, and that may well be a distinctive and particular feature of Christianity.[14] But is that to say that Jesus is the only means by which humanity experiences the reality of God? Surely, some modesty is called for whenever we speak of the great mystery of God. Moreover, John's unique presentation of Jesus as the Cosmic Christ should give us pause. Alan Culpepper explains why:

The Gospel's opening gambit is to describe the work of the Logos by drawing from the Wisdom tradition. As Wisdom, the Logos was the creative agent. Wisdom manifests God's design and power in all the creation. . . .

The exclusivist claims of the Fourth Gospel . . . must therefore be understood in the context of the opening claim that the revelation that came through Jesus Christ is the same as that which is universally present in the Logos. . . .

Because the Gospel presents Jesus as the incarnation who made known the work of the Logos from the creation and through all time, it undercuts the triumphalism of claims that Christendom has a monopoly on the revelation of God. . . . Accordingly, John's Logos Christology allows Christians to affirm that adherents of other religious traditions may come to know God through the work of the Cosmic Christ.[15]

May all of these observations provide food for thought as we wrestle with the problems and possibilities that this particular "I AM" saying presents.

"I AM THE VINE, YOU ARE THE BRANCHES" (15:1–11)

Finally, consider one of John's most unique images of the relationship that exists between Jesus and the church: "I am the vine, you are the branches. Those who abide in me and I in them bear much fruit, because apart from me you can do nothing" (15:5). The image of Jesus as the life-giving vine conveys, perhaps more clearly than any other, his intimate, animating role in the lives of believers, who depend upon him completely for the gift of life. By the end of the first century, other New Testament writers imaged the relationship quite differently, picturing Jesus as the church's builder, founder, or cornerstone (Matt. 16:18; Eph. 2:20). As Raymond Brown points out, those other images contain important insights but suffer from "the limitations of constructional language,"[16] for is there not a difference between a vine and a cornerstone? A cornerstone relates Jesus to the church as one who is past or as an inert presence. John, however, describes Jesus as the animating principle of the Christian community, still alive and well in its midst.[17] This point is further underlined by marked repetition of one of John's favorite verbs, "abide"—a verb that conveys constancy of presence. Those who abide in Jesus, the vine, are sustained in a relationship of trust, love, knowledge, and oneness characteristic of God and Christ.

The image of the vine and branches is remarkable in one further respect: it is an astonishingly nonhierarchical—even antihierarchical—depiction of the church. As commentator Gail O'Day observes, on a vine "one branch is indistinguishable from another; no branch has pride of place. . . . There is no bishop branch, elder branch, or church bureaucrat branch with special status in this vine. One cannot distinguish between clergy and laity in this vine."[18] All are rooted together in the one vine, and entwined with one another in a community of mutuality and interrelationship. Bound to Jesus (the vine) and to one another, believers are "pruned" and empowered to grow in faith and to bear much "fruit"—which, for John, is love (see 15:9–17).

In conclusion, note that as we hear Jesus interpret who he is through myriad images, we are also hearing the voice of the early Christian community confessing its faith in him. What is Jesus in their experience and ours? He is the one who nourishes us in the midst of our journey, who leads us out of darkness and illumines our path. Indeed, he himself is the way to God. He is our shepherd, who gathers us into a beloved flock where we are intimately known and leads us into pastures of abundant life. Clinging to him and to one another, we thrive, blossom, and bear fruit of love. In sum, Jesus is God's gift of life!

QUESTIONS FOR DISCUSSION OR REFLECTION

Read aloud 6:35–59; 8:12; 9:4–5; 10:1–18; 14:1–7; and 15:1–11. Following the reading, share briefly: What most captures your attention as you consider the images used to describe who Jesus is and what he represents in the lives of believers? What questions do they raise for you?

Of all the images of life discussed in this chapter—bread, light, door, shepherd, way, vine and branches—which most powerfully depicts what God in Christ and the Christian community have represented in your own experience, and why? Which image has the greatest appeal for you, and why?

If there are bread bakers in your group, ask them to share what the image of bread evokes for them.

Jesus' words (especially in 6:52–58) call to mind his presence to us in the Lord's Supper, which is indeed a means by which we continue to receive a share in God's own life. Is regular participation in the Lord's Supper a meaningful part of your faith experience? Why, or why not?

What is your deepest hunger? How have you been nourished in the midst of your journey by your experience of God in Christ?

How has the one who identified himself as "the light of the world" changed your vision of the world around you? How do you, as his disciple, now see it differently?

Share your impressions: do you think people experience your congregation and your denomination as "open-door" communities? Why, or why not?

Some in your group may actually have experience with sheep. Ask them to share their insights into the nature of the imagery of "sheep" and "shepherd."

What does the image of Jesus as the good shepherd mean to you? What memories or impressions does it evoke?

Has Jesus' "I AM" saying in 14:6 ("I am the way") been a controversial one in your experience? Why, or why not? How would you articulate your understanding of it?

Some in your group may have more gardening experience and knowledge of "vines and branches" than others. Ask them to share their insights into the nature of this imagery.

What does the description of the Christian community in terms of a vine and its branches contribute to your understanding of the church? What does it suggest about your relationship to God in Christ and to other believers?

What new insights have you gained from your study and discussion of the images of life in the Gospel of John?

Note: one final "I AM" saying ("I am the resurrection and the life" in 11:25) will be considered in chapter 8 of this study.

6

Between a Rock and a Hard Place: A Woman Accused of Adultery

John 7:53–8:11

From its earliest history, the church has been ill at ease with matters of sexual impropriety. The text before us is a case in point. Scholars generally agree that the story of "the woman caught in adultery" was not originally part of the Gospel of John (for this reason, you may find it enclosed in double brackets in your Bible, or omitted altogether). It does not appear in the earliest Greek manuscripts of John; it is more characteristic of Luke than John in vocabulary, style, and theology; and it interrupts the narrative in progress (you can skip from 7:52 to 8:12 without missing a beat). In later Greek manuscripts, the story appears in various locations: after 7:36, 7:52, 21:25, even after Luke 21:38. It is a truly homeless story. However, scholars also believe that the story is a truly ancient one based on the earliest oral traditions about Jesus, a story that has all the earmarks of an authentic incident from his life. Why, then, did it become a free-floating story without a secure canonical home? In all likelihood, because it was suppressed! The ease with which Jesus extended mercy to an adulterous woman embarrassed the earliest Christian communities and undermined their own more severe penitential practices.[1] Moreover, many interpreters (ancient and modern) have feared that Christian women would find encouragement in the story to live unchaste lives—to "sin with impunity."[2]

Nevertheless, the power of the story is such that it has been cherished and preserved through the centuries and is worthy of our close attention. Indeed, New Testament scholar Raymond Brown observes, "No

51

apology is needed for this once independent story which has found its way into the Fourth Gospel and some manuscripts of Luke, for in quality and beauty it is worthy of either localization. . . . And the delicate balance between the justice of Jesus in not condoning the sin and his mercy in forgiving the sinner is one of the great gospel lessons."[3]

The unnamed woman, however, is not the only sinner who encounters Jesus in this story, or who hears a promise of new life. That the story is traditionally referred to as "the woman caught in adultery" tends to focus our attention solely on the woman and issues of sexual sin and obscures the significant role that others, too, play in this scene. Religious persons and groups who would judge and condemn the one guilty of sexual sin are also addressed by Jesus—in strikingly parallel fashion[4]— and they too find their lives graced and transformed by the Word made flesh. Indeed, as Gail O'Day has demonstrated, the story unfolds in two parallel scenes in which Jesus bends down and writes on the ground (vv. 6, 8). Then Jesus stands up to speak to his conversation partners, first to the scribes and Pharisees in verse 7, and then to the woman in verse 10a. Finally, Jesus addresses words about sin to them both, to the scribes and Pharisees in verse 7c, and to the woman in verse 11b.[5] Let us look closely at both dimensions of this story.

SINNERS ENCOUNTER JESUS

The story is set in the temple precincts, where Jesus is interrupted as he teaches: "The scribes and the Pharisees brought a woman who had been caught in adultery; and making her stand before all of them, they said to him, 'Teacher, this woman was caught in the very act of committing adultery. Now in the law Moses commanded us to stone such women. Now what do you say?'" (vv. 3–5).

What's wrong with this picture? For one thing, where is the man who has been caught with the woman "in the very act of committing adultery"? Is his absence a reflection of the perennial double standard associated with women's sexuality? Or even an indication that the woman has been entrapped? Other irregularities appear as well. The religious authorities speak of only half the law of Moses, for they advise that it required them "to stone such women," when in fact the law prescribed the death penalty for both the man and woman involved (see Lev. 20:10; Deut. 22:22–24). Nor are witnesses produced who could verify the charge. Clearly, neither the law nor the woman is the real focus of concern. Indeed, "They said this to test him, so that they might have some charge to bring against him" (John 8:6).

How does Jesus respond to what is, in effect, a challenge to join a lynch mob in rendering judgment, to take part in a stoning? His first response is nonverbal: "Jesus bent down and wrote with his finger on the ground" (v. 6). We are not told what Jesus writes on the ground, and therefore speculation abounds. Recently, in a Bible study, a woman told me she knew exactly what Jesus was writing: "It takes two!" Others maintain that Jesus simply doodles to contain his anger or to buy time for reflection; still others imagine that he writes out either the sins of the accusers or words of Scripture, perhaps the Ten Commandments, Jeremiah 17:13 ("those who turn away from [me] shall be recorded in the underworld, for they have forsaken the fountain of living water, the LORD"), or Exodus 23:1b, 7 ("You shall not join hands with the wicked to act as a malicious witness. . . . Keep far from a false charge, and do not kill the innocent and those in the right, for I will not acquit the guilty"). This is the only place in the New Testament where Jesus is presented as writing, which explains, in part, why scholars have been overly concerned to identify what he writes. But their efforts no doubt also reflect discomfort with the narrative, as Gail O'Day contends: "Attempts to find the interpretive key to John 7:53–8:11 in something outside the given story reveal a dissatisfaction with and distrust of the story as it is written. Such interpretations constitute a refusal to take the text seriously."[6]

Moreover, to fill in the blank is to miss the import of a dramatic action that speaks louder than words. By lowering himself, and thus refusing to stand with them, Jesus offers a visible sign of disengagement. As Patricia Klindienst Joplin observes: "The gesture functions structurally: Jesus bends down to break the spell of unanimity generated among the crowd of men all of whom stand up, as one, before him. . . . The point is, he physically distinguishes his position from theirs. . . . He not only refuses to stand with the accusers, he lowers himself, uncontaminated by the crowd's desire or the very dirt he draws in, a sign of our common origin and end."[7] Luise Schottroff contends that his gesture is also an "act of civil courage": "He resists the pressure of the group and of the presumably hysterical atmosphere of the stoning and refuses for himself to condemn and stone the woman."[8]

Another perspective on Jesus' dramatic action is offered by Rowan Williams in his reflection on the events of September 11, 2001, entitled *Writing in the Dust: After September 11*. Williams was present in Manhattan on that morning when the Twin Towers of the World Trade Center fell, which accounts in part for the title he chose for his book; but it was also evoked by Jesus' action of writing with his finger on the ground in John 8:

> What on earth is he doing? . . . There is one meaning that seems to me obvious in the light of what I think we learned that morning. He hesitates. He does not draw a line, fix an interpretation, tell the woman who she is and what her fate should be. He allows a moment, a longish moment, in which people are given time to see themselves differently precisely because he refuses to make the sense they want. When he lifts his head, there is both judgement and release.[9]

Thus Williams describes his own reflection as "writing in the dust because it tries to hold that moment for a little longer, long enough for some of our demons to walk away."[10] This thoughtful perspective on Jesus' nonverbal response points up the deep wisdom of it.

Nevertheless, Jesus' inquisitors persist in their challenge: "they kept on questioning him" (v. 7). Thus he provides a verbal response as well: "he straightened up and said to them, 'Let anyone among you who is without sin be the first to throw a stone at her.' And once again he bent down and wrote on the ground" (vv. 7–8). Jesus' stunning counterchallenge quite literally disarms a mob and is noteworthy in two important respects. First, it indicates that Jesus refuses to rank or order sins. He is not overly fascinated with sexual sin; nor does he seem to regard it as greater than other sins in the sight of God. Second, his counterchallenge is addressed to individuals rather than to an undifferentiated crowd and directs their gaze inward, where they may discern from their own personal histories whether they are truly in a position to condemn.[11] To their credit, none accepts the invitation to cast the first stone. None exempts himself from self-judgment.[12] Indeed, we ought not to presume that they make a shameful exit from the scene, slinking off with their tail between their legs. Though they had arrived on the scene as an undifferentiated mob, they depart "one by one" (v. 9), as individuals who have been disarmed and redirected by the self-knowledge that emerges in encounter with the Word.

The woman finds herself left alone with Jesus, and for the first time in the story she is personally addressed and summoned to speech: "Jesus straightened up and said to her, 'Woman, where are they? Has no one condemned you?' She said, 'No one, sir.' And Jesus said, 'Neither do I condemn you. Go your way, and from now on do not sin again'" (vv. 10–11). As Gail O'Day observes, Jesus treats both the religious authorities and the woman as "theological equals, each as human beings to whom words about sin can be addressed."[13] Moreover, "Both the scribes and Pharisees and the woman are invited to give up old ways and enter a new way of life."[14] Though at the story's beginning she was a condemned woman, surrounded and threatened by violence, at its end she finds herself a free woman—free to go and to amend her ways. She is not to be imprisoned by her past, for the one before her refuses to let the guilt of sin define us and directs us toward an open future.

LINGERING QUESTIONS

The text presents a number of lingering questions, perhaps especially about the woman at the center of the episode whose circumstances are shrouded in silence, but also about the scribes and Pharisees. Indeed, it may be important to examine our presuppositions about them.

Many of us read Gospel narratives expecting that the Jewish leaders will be cast in the role of villains, as they often are, opposing Jesus and seeking his destruction. Indeed, in this story, their motivation in bringing the case of the adulteress before him is explicitly noted: "They said this to test him, so that they might have some charge to bring against him" (v. 6). This evaluative aside from the narrator provides damning commentary that guides the reader to a negative assessment of the scribes' and Pharisees' motivation. But what if verse 6a was not a part of the story? Would not the story read quite differently without it?

Brad H. Young, a scholar with special interest in first-century Judaism, has explored this possibility.[15] He observes, first, that 8:6a is textually suspect, that a number of scholars have questioned whether it was originally included in ancient Greek manuscripts containing the story. He also traces a century-long debate about 8:6a, noting that many preeminent scholars have regarded the verse as a gloss or interpolation, that is, as an extraneous note or comment that later scribes or copyists have incorporated right into the biblical text.

Young raises significant historical questions that further call into question the standard reading of the Pharisees here as a lynch mob, eager to use the death penalty against the adulteress and to entrap Jesus. He notes, "many of these traditional readings of the story of the adulteress seem in conflict with what is known about Pharisaic attitudes and practices from both non-Christian sources such as Josephus or rabbinic literature as well as from a NT source such as Luke-Acts."[16] For example, Josephus, a first-century Jewish historian, tells us that Pharisees sought to avoid using the death penalty and were "naturally lenient in the matter of punishments" (*Antiquities* 13.294). New Testament evidence is also pertinent. In Luke 13:31 the Pharisees warn Jesus that Herod Antipas desires to kill him, and in Acts 5:33–39 the great Pharisaic teacher Gamaliel argues strongly for the defense of Peter and John, saving the lives of the apostles. Young concludes, "In all events, the historical sources indicate that the Pharisees were reluctant to use capital punishment."[17]

These thoughts lead Young to an interesting possibility: "Maybe the Pharisees had no intention of accusing Jesus at all. Perhaps they wanted to help the accused woman. When it becomes clear that John 8:6a is an addition to the text, the question of the Pharisees may be viewed from a fresh perspective."[18] Young suggests that the episode in 7:53–8:11 (once 8:6a is removed) actually describes a frequent occurrence in Jewish life: "When a difficult religious issue arises in the life of the community which affects faith and practice, it was an accepted custom to seek a *responsum*."[19] A responsum provided a forum in which questions and answers became a foundation of establishing accepted custom and official jurisprudence. Indeed, as Young notes, "Seeking answers to questions concerning biblical interpretation is a crucial part of the Jewish religious experience."[20]

How does this inform a reading of 7:53–8:11? In Young's view,

> The Pharisees had a problem. The evidence against the woman was irrefutable. The Pharisees, however, did not want to execute her, but the law of Moses taught that an adulteress should be stoned to death. On the one hand they wanted to obey the law, but on the other, they wished to save her life. In an effort to accomplish two aims, they sought to find a loophole in the interpretation of the Torah which would guarantee her release or at least a more lenient and just ruling in her case. When they learned that Jesus, a young teacher with innovative ideas and a popular following, was in the Temple, they believed that he might be of assistance. As a recognized teacher coming from Galilee, he might possess fresh insight. The Pharisees decided to seek a *responsum* from Jesus.[21]

Thus in 7:53–8:11 the scribes and Pharisees ask Jesus a valid question relating to the interpretation of the Torah. Jesus writes in the dirt, and then gives his answer in an oral form that challenges the listeners with the higher purpose of the Torah. Young observes that "the whole episode portrays the oral tradition as a living Torah which is adapted and applied in everyday life situations. Such a view is very close to the Pharisees'."[22]

Moreover, he interprets the writing on the ground as a parabolic action signaling the fact that the oral law did not require written proof. When Jesus utters his wise and famous response, "Let anyone among you who is without sin be the first to throw a stone at her," the Pharisees apparently agree and accept his ruling. "It is doubtful," he observes, "that a lynch mob would be moved by such a remark."[23] In sum, he notes, "His reply is enough for the Pharisees, who are quite liberal in their innovative approaches designed to give application of the law in their daily lives. They wanted to save her and Jesus helped them."[24]

There is, of course, no way of proving the matter. But our understanding of the Pharisees is greatly in need of revision. The caricatures and stereotypes that have so often characterized our descriptions of them have been unduly influenced by early Christian polemics inscribed in the New Testament and do not always authentically reflect the Pharisaic historical reality. Given the sad Christian history of anti-Judaic interpretation, Young's alternative perspective provides a salutary question mark to linger in the corners of our minds.

We also need to examine our presuppositions about the woman in 7:53–8:11. The Pharisees, Jesus, and most readers of the story all appear to share the assumption that she has in fact committed adultery. She is described, after all, as having been "caught in the very act" (8:4). However, no witnesses are produced to verify this claim, nor a partner in crime, and we are not made privy to her own reflections on what has transpired. The woman is not given a chance to speak in her own defense. We do not hear her voice until the end of the story, when Jesus asks if anyone remains to condemn her (to which she responds briefly, "No one, Lord") and sends her on her way with an admonition not to sin again.

Given that the story provides no further details about the woman's circumstances, an appropriate assumption may well be that the accused has committed adultery. Our purpose is not to dispute this claim, but rather to acknowledge the paltry information about her, and also to stretch our imaginations to consider whether there might not be other possibilities residing in the silences of the story and between its lines.

Given the dubious legalities represented in the scene (no trial, no witnesses, no partner in crime, and noninclusive reference to a law that includes *both* women and men in its purview), some interpreters have found cause to wonder if the woman might have been entrapped.[25] Others detect intertextual echoes of the story of Susanna, an apocryphal addition to the book of Daniel, in which the young, wise Daniel intervenes to save a beautiful woman who has been condemned to death for adultery on the testimony of two false witnesses, lecherous elders of the Jews who have been rebuffed in their attempt to seduce her.[26]

Jean K. Kim also attends to the woman's circumstances, stretching our minds further with sociohistorical analysis that provides a compelling accounting of silences in the story.[27] Reading from a postcolonial perspective, Kim reminds us that Israel was a colonized nation, occupied by Roman military forces. Then, as now in military base areas such as Okinawa, Subic Bay in the Philippines, and South Korea, "sexually oppressed women are caught in a no-win situation between foreign and native men."[28] Moreover, when crimes are committed, occupying forces enjoy immunity from local prosecution. Thus in Kim's view the colonizing domination of the Roman Empire may explain why there is no mention of the man caught in adultery:

> From this historical point of view, if the adulterer was a Roman soldier (as we might assume), the Pharisees, scribes, and even Jesus could not do anything to accuse him because he, as a powerful patron, was beyond their control. In a patriarchal society, woman has thus been simply the ground on which competing views of tradition or national identity are debated. In other words, it was only as a site of (im)purity that she was brought to the debate scene in order that the legitimate authority of the colonized Israel might be contested.[29]

Kim's reading leaves us pondering the silences in the story with very disturbing questions.

One final perspective on the woman's circumstance, from Alan Watson, provides additional food for thought.[30] It is also an argument from silence, but one that is plausible. Watson, considering the possibility that the woman may have been a remarried divorcée, places the story in a specific historical context: "Jesus had declared that a woman whose husband had divorced her and who remarried committed adultery (Matt. 5:31–32; 19:3–9; Mark 10:2–9)."[31] Thus, by Jesus' own claim, a remarried divorcée would have been an adulteress:

> Moses allowed divorce, Jesus forbade it. The trap of the Pharisees was this: the law of Moses demanded death by stoning for an adulteress; Jesus claimed remarried divorcées were adulteresses though Moses did not, and neither did the Pharisees. Would Jesus follow his argument to its logical conclusion and impose death on a remarried divorcée? The scribes and Pharisees brought the woman to Jesus very precisely to test him.[32]

Jesus had widened the scope of adultery and is thus "caught in a trap he himself had made."[33] How does he manage to escape it? By singling out an individual, and transferring the possible crime of the adulteress to the sin of the husband who divorced her: "The one among you who is without sin (*anamartētos*), let him cast the first stone at her." Watson reads the Greek *anamartētos* as singular—"the one among you who is without sin"; it does not mean "anyone."[34] It is important to remember that in Jewish law divorce proceeds from the husband.

The fascinating aspect of Watson's argument is that it does explain many of the troubling features of the story, for example, why the woman has not been formally tried or condemned for her crime; why Jesus accepts that she is guilty; why no evidence or witnesses are produced, nor a partner in crime; and why the woman is brought by the scribes and Pharisees to Jesus. For the Pharisees, there was no adultery, no catching in the act, and no male adulterer.

Why, then, does the text never explicitly state that the woman was a remarried divorcée? Watson speculates that as this story circulated orally among early Christians, "It presented problems that would be blurred in oral repetition. First, Jesus would appear more loving and forgiving if the context were generalized. Second, Jesus would not appear to be faced with a strong moral and legal dilemma of his own making if the context were generalized."[35] Indeed, the complicated textual history of the story may reflect "discomfort with the episode, an unwillingness to ignore it yet a reluctance to accept it."[36] Watson's scenario thus provides, in his view, "a plausible early setting" for the story, and an explanation of "why the pericope was changed yet retained."[37]

Again, we are faced with an argument that cannot be proved one way or the other. But we are also left with significant questions to ponder in our ongoing engagement with this story.

CONTEMPORARY IMPLICATIONS

The implications of the story are many. There may be no doubt that the whole of the biblical witness identifies adultery as sin and does not condone it. There is also no question that we live in a society that commonly judges sexual behavior more harshly than any other sin, the church being no exception. Both of these realities are addressed in a wise book by Baptist minister C. Welton Gaddy entitled *Adultery and Grace: The Ultimate Scandal.* In that book, Gaddy treats adultery as sin, a manifestation of human brokenness in need of God's forgiving and redeeming power. But he also takes churches to task:

> All too often, institutions of religion, notably local churches—ostensibly dispensaries of grace—compound the problems and intensify the trauma that plague people who have committed adultery. Ministers preach biblical grace, but practice vengeful judgment. Congregations invite "any and all" people to experience God's forgiveness, but turn away from their fellowships individuals guilty of "morals" charges. Undistinguished from other social bodies in this matter, the church tends to treat adultery as a sin so terrible that applying grace to it is unimaginable, thus demonstrating a scandalous misunderstanding of sin, adultery, and grace.[38]

Gaddy maintains that "to withhold grace and forgiveness from people guilty of adultery (or for persons guilty of adultery to withhold grace and forgiveness from themselves) constitutes a wrong equal in its severity to that of adultery."[39] He argues in the spirit of John 8: "Grace refuses to allow an episode of adultery to serve as the ultimate commentary on a person's character. Without in any way condoning the sin of adultery, grace seeks to halt negative reactions to an adulterer and create an opportunity for that person to enjoy a life that changes for the better."[40] His observations provide significant food for thought for the Christian community as it wrestles with sin, judgment, and forgiveness—issues of enduring importance to people of faith.

Other implications emerge when we consider the far-reaching effects of judgmentalism in human life. Church historian Roberta Bondi speaks of judgmentalism as one of the fundamental struggles of the Christian life:

> Judgmentalism destroys community; it destroys those who do the judging, and, even more seriously, . . . it often destroys (and certainly excludes from community) the one who is judged. On a small scale judgmentalism destroys marriages, families, and churches. On a wider scale it provides the major fuel of racism, sexism, neglect of the poor, and national self-righteousness. Judgmentalism for this reason as a breach of love is as serious as any other sin we might commit against one another.[41]

How are we freed from a judging spirit? The story in John 8 suggests that self-knowledge plays a crucial role. Informed by the teachings of the early monastic writers, Bondi concurs:

*Cultivating the virtue of seeing ourselves as sinners is a major source of
healing the wounds of judgmentalism in our hearts.* . . . Knowing that
I am a sinner means taking seriously the knowledge that we all do or
at least are capable of terrible things. The monastic teachers were
quite certain that it is not possible to love other people unless we
understand at a very deep level that our human failings in the area of
love put us all in the same boat.[42]

To know ourselves as sinners, and thereby to heal our judgmental hearts,
would appear to be foundational to our ability to extend ourselves in
love and compassion to others, and perhaps also to ourselves. We share
a common human struggle with sin, and are indeed all in the same
boat—equally reliant on God's grace.

Susan Brooks Thistlethwaite, a minister and scholar who has worked
with battered women, highlights another contemporary dimension of
this ancient story. She observes that it is the biblical text with which
many abused women find the most identification: "Women who have
suffered physical violence hear that whatever human law or custom may
legitimate violence against women, it cannot stand face to face with the
revelation of God's affirmation of all humanity. Many abused women
would echo the joy of the woman who exclaimed, 'That's right! He
[Jesus] broke the law for her!'"[43]

For these and many other reasons we may be grateful that Christians
through the ages have treasured and preserved this ancient, homeless
story, and that it has found a tentative resting place in John. May it continue to bear witness to the one who redeems lives that have been disfigured by a judgmental spirit, as well as lives that have been disfigured
by more self-evident expressions of sin. There can scarcely be any better illustration of Paul's affirmation that anyone in Christ is a "new creation: everything old has passed away; see, everything has become new!"
(2 Cor. 5:17). Our lives are given back to us with hope, for in the name
of Jesus Christ our sins are forgiven.

QUESTIONS FOR DISCUSSION OR REFLECTION

Do a dramatic reading of John 7:53–8:11. Assign roles to a narrator, to Jesus, and to the woman. Have the rest of the group read
collectively the lines of the scribes and Pharisees. It is helpful to
see the story as well as hear it, so also ask participants to stand

in a circle with Jesus and the woman in the middle, and include Jesus' physical movements in the dramatic reading. Following the reading, share briefly: What most captures your attention as you hear the story? What questions does the story raise for you?

One of the features of the story that is uncharacteristic of John is an understanding of sin that is linked to actions. The Fourth Gospel more typically links sin and unbelief. Sin is the refusal to recognize Jesus as the revelation of God (see 3:17–21; 8:24; 16:9). Still, one can argue that the story has found an appropriate resting place, for women are featured prominently in John, and the story illustrates key themes of the dialogues in John 7–8. You may wish to examine some of the thematic connections in 7:19–24, 48–49, 51; 8:15–16, 46. Does it matter to you that the story was not originally part of the Gospel of John? Why or why not? What difference does it make, in your view?

With whom do you identify in this story, and why? Where have you encountered realities represented in the story in your own experience? How can the story inform your own practice of Christian discipleship and community?

How would you interpret Jesus' enigmatic gesture of writing on the ground?

Have you ever had an experience in which a gesture or posture may have spoken louder than words?

What do you make of the fact that only the woman caught "in the very act of committing adultery" is brought before Jesus?

The crowd disperses "one by one, beginning with the elders" (v. 9). Why do you think the elders were the first to leave?

Why do you think sexual misconduct is commonly judged more harshly than any other sin in both church and society? Should it be?

Do you think judgmentalism is a breach of love as serious as any other sin we might commit against one another? Why or why not?

What is your response to C. Welton Gaddy's observations? To those of Roberta Bondi? To those of Susan Brooks Thistlethwaite? What other contemporary implications of this ancient story come to mind?

What are your presuppositions about the scribes and Pharisees as you hear this story?

What are your presuppositions about the accused woman? What do you imagine her circumstances to have been?

As noted, the story is not simply one of "a woman caught in adultery," though it has traditionally carried this title. How would you retitle the story to reflect more accurately its dynamics? See if you can come up with a better title.

What new insights have emerged from your consideration or discussion together of this story?

7

A Journey to Sight: The Man Born Blind

John 9

One of the most vivid images that Jesus uses to speak of who he is and what he represents in the lives of believers is the image of light: "I am the light of the world. Whoever follows me will never walk in darkness but will have the light of life" (8:12). The image conveys his singular role as revealer—the one through whom God's light shines, and the one who illumines the meaning and purpose of human life. Jesus' use of this image has important implications for discipleship as well. Our response to the light of God manifest in Christ has implications for how we walk, that is, for how we live. Light can illumine our path and our walking. However, if we obstinately stare at it and refuse to recognize its power, we can be blinded.[1] All of these dimensions of the image find powerful expression in one of John's most dramatic stories: the healing of a man blind from birth (chap. 9). At its beginning, Jesus claims once again: "As long as I am in the world, I am the light of the world" (9:5). Then, in demonstration of this role, he opens the eyes of the blind man. But as the story unfolds, it provides a penetrating study of spiritual sight and spiritual blindness, inviting us to examine the state of our own vision.

WHO SINNED? (9:1–7)

The episode opens when the disciples spot a man blind from birth and ask Jesus a peculiar theological question: "Rabbi, who sinned, this man or his parents, that he was born blind?" (9:2). We may find the question

objectionable, presuming, as it does, a causal link between tragic misfortune and sin, and even the possibility of prenatal sin in the case of
congenital blindness. Despite the book of Job's refutation of any such
link, the notion of it was alive and well in Jesus' day (e.g., Luke 13:2).
To be honest, it is alive and well in ours, too, whenever anyone asks,
"What did I [or they] do to deserve this?"—trying to make sense of
painful human experience. Jesus, however, refuses to pursue this line of
questioning, resisting analysis of the situation in any such terms: "Neither this man nor his parents sinned; he was born blind so that God's
works might be revealed in him" (9:3). At first glance, Jesus' response
has its own difficulties. Has God inflicted a lifetime of blindness upon
this poor soul in order to stage a dramatic demonstration of divine
power? But translation difficulties attend this verse. The words "he was
born blind" in the NRSV's translation do not actually appear in the
Greek text, but are rather supplied by translators to make sense of a
seemingly incomplete sentence. (The NIV translates in similar fashion:
"'Neither this man nor his parents sinned,' said Jesus, '*This happened* so
that the work of God might be displayed in his life.'") However, repunc-
tuation of verses 3–4 renders a quite different reading: "Neither this
man nor his parents sinned, but in order that the works of God might
be revealed in him, we must work the works of him who sent me. . . ."[2]

Whatever the case may be, the unanswered question, "Who sinned?"
hangs over the whole episode that follows. Perhaps the disciples' question springs from the quite human anxiety to secure their own existence,
to assure themselves that they live in a just, predictable, and orderly
world: if an avoidable cause (or sin) can be identified for such misfortune, then they (and we) can all rest easier. But by abstracting the situation, by looking upon the man as an object of curiosity and theological
speculation, they evade commitment and action that might relieve
human misery.[3] Jesus refocuses their attention on the real issue at hand.
In short, "stop asking abstract moral questions and get about the business of healing!"[4] Such business is essential to discipleship, for the healing of the world is God's own mission, a mission to which Jesus commits
himself and in which he explicitly includes his disciples ("*We* must work
the works of him who sent me").

The mission is an urgent one, for Jesus' time in the world is limited
("night is coming"). Thus the miracle unfolds quickly as he spits on the
ground, makes mud with the saliva, spreads it on the blind man's eyes,
and sends him to a pool to wash. The blind man may well have been familiar with human spittle upon his face (see 9:8), but Jesus' act, reminiscent

of God's creation of humanity from the dust of the earth (Gen. 2), takes on the aura of re-creation. Moreover, the pool in which the man is sent to wash is named "Siloam (which means Sent)" (9:7). As Jesus in John describes himself repeatedly as one "sent" from God (9:4; see also 7:28–29; 10:36; 12:45), we are meant to identify the pool somehow with Jesus and given to understand that the blind man, by washing in water, is plunged into Jesus' own life—that his cure resides not in the waters but in his contact with the Sent One.[5] The washing in water itself takes place offstage, and we are not observers of the moment in which sight is restored. Instead, we witness the moment of return when the man "came back able to see" (9:7).

Interestingly, we do not hear the blind man's voice in this opening scene. He does not cry out in faith or in need for mercy and healing (e.g., Mark 10:46–52). The healing takes place solely at Jesus' initiative and is unconditional—an act of pure grace. But once acted upon, the man responds in obedience to Jesus' command (9:7). Moreover, his story does not end here. The miracle unfolds quickly, in two verses, but the consequences of it consume 33 verses to follow, providing an opportunity to follow the man's more demanding journey to faith and inner sight in the aftermath of his healing.

A JOURNEY TO INNER SIGHT (9:8–41)

The remarkable gift of sight does not evoke wonder, joy, thanksgiving, or praise on the part of those who learn of it, but rather confusion, consternation, and controversy. Arguments break out, first as the formerly blind man encounters perplexed neighbors and others who had known him before, and then as he is brought before religious authorities for an official investigation of the healing. Thus a widening cast of characters embodies a variety of flustered responses to both the healer and the healing.

As neighbors and others encounter the formerly blind man, we learn something new about him: that blindness had rendered him destitute, reduced him to panhandling, for they wonder, "Is this not the man who used to sit and beg?" (9:8). Perhaps they had paid so little attention to him that they cannot be sure. Even now they do not inquire directly with him about this, but rather dispute the matter among themselves, airing divided opinions, until the man intrudes upon their conversation, declaring repeatedly, "I am the man," or, translating literally, "I AM"

(9:9). Only here in the Fourth Gospel do the dramatic words "I AM" (*egō eimi* in Greek) appear on the lips of anyone other than Jesus, who uses them repeatedly in ways that link his very being with the God revealed to Moses in the burning bush (Exod. 3:13–14; see John 4:26; 6:20, 35, 48; 8:12, 28, 58; 9:5; 10:7, 11, 14; 11:25; 13:19; 14:6; 15:1, 5; 18:5–6). Indeed, there is a sense in which the formerly blind man now functions as a surrogate for Jesus, an *alter Christus* of sorts.[6] He is, after all, now identified with Jesus, having been immersed in the life of the Sent One. Moreover, when asked how his eyes were opened, he speaks (literally) of Jesus' "anointing" (*epechrisen* in Greek) of them, conveying, perhaps, that he has been chosen and sent forth. Whatever the case may be, he provides a remarkably detailed recounting of his healing (9:11). Clearly, though he was blind and silent, he was by no means deaf, and was paying close attention to everything happening to him. He even knows the name of his healer. But asked of Jesus' whereabouts, he must say "I do not know" (9:12). How could he—he has never seen Jesus, and will not encounter him again until the end of this story.

It is Jesus' longest absence in this decidedly christocentric Gospel— the only point at which he steps offstage for an extended period of time. He remains the constant focus of conversation and controversy, but his twenty-seven-verse absence from the narrative is unusual. Moreover, the unusual spotlight given his surrogate, a disciple in the making, as he contends with ordeals suggests that the story may have been an important one for the community to which the Fourth Gospel was first addressed. Indeed, John 9 proved to be the key that finally cracked the puzzle of the Johannine community, revealing something of the difficult historical circumstances that the Gospel first addressed.[7] The man born blind appears to function as a hero of John's first-century community, embodying in his story a difficult journey that the community itself had taken. Like him, these Christians had found their eyes opened by the one who is the light of the world. As a result, they found themselves under intense scrutiny, even suffering expulsion from the synagogue for their confession of faith (9:22; 12:42; 16:2), which eventually proves to be the formerly blind man's fate (9:34). Thus his story both informed and fortified their own.

We are not told why the neighbors bring the blind man before the Pharisees, but for whatever reason, unable to settle the matter themselves, they seek the intervention of learned religious authorities, "men of mature judgment."[8] An official investigation is thus set in motion and the formerly blind man is asked to recount his experience a second time.

Initially, the Pharisees, like the neighbors, find themselves divided in opinion, though their debate centers not on the identity of the blind man but on the identity of his healer. Moreover, their quandary is triggered by a new bit of information, for we learn at this point that Jesus' healing of the man born blind took place on a Sabbath day (9:14). Healing on the Sabbath was, of course, allowed in cases of emergency if life were in danger; but from their perspective, unaware as they are of the urgency of Jesus' mission (9:4) and his divine prerogative (5:16–30), the healing of one congenitally blind could easily have waited another day. Additionally, Jesus' "kneading" of clay places him in violation of one of thirty-nine categories of work forbidden on the Sabbath. So what are learned legal scholars to conclude from these transgressions? Some Pharisees surmise that Jesus could not be from God. But others wonder, "How can a man who is a sinner perform such signs?" (9:16). So turning to the formerly blind man, they ask again, "What do you say about him? It was your eyes he opened." And amid all the wrangling and reflection on his experience the man has apparently arrived at a moment of insight: "He is a prophet" (9:17).

The investigation then takes a dramatic turn at its center. Though the religious authorities had initially appeared to accept that a miracle had taken place, they now raise doubts about that. The man's parents are summoned and intimidated by insinuations of collusion in a hoax: "Is this your son, who you say was born blind? How then does he now see?" (9:19). In response to the first question, the parents confirm that the man is their son and that he was born blind, but profess ignorance with respect to the second question, about the healing. They also claim ignorance with respect to a third matter about which they were not asked: the identity of the healer. Clearly, they know more than they let on. But in a chilling display of moral cowardice, they direct the attention of the authorities back to their son: "Ask him; he is of age. He will speak for himself" (9:21).

Their diversionary tactic is prompted by fear: "His parents said this because they were afraid of the Jews; for the Jews had already agreed that anyone who confessed Jesus to be the Messiah would be put out of the synagogue" (9:22). This explanation of their motivation, the longest attribution of intention in the Fourth Gospel to this point,[9] is the most important bit of evidence we have of the circumstances of the community to which it was first addressed, signaled by the fact that anachronism abounds. For one thing, expulsion of Christians from synagogues did not take place during Jesus' life and ministry. Only after the destruction of the Temple in 70 CE did Jews and Jewish Christians find themselves in a painful family quarrel and a difficult process of self-differentiation. The reference to expulsion from the synagogue in 9:22 and 34, along with two further explicit references in 12:42 and 16:2, suggests that John's community included Jewish Christians who, in their particular locale, had suffered expulsion from the synagogue for their confession of faith in Jesus Christ. After expulsion they would no longer have considered themselves Jews, which explains another odd feature of the story: the parents of the man born blind are described as being "afraid of the Jews," even though they themselves are Jews, as are their son and Jesus. As Raymond Brown notes, this is "just as awkward as having an American living in Washington, DC, described as being afraid of 'the Americans.'"[10] Such a reference makes sense only in a post–70 CE setting, as does interchangeable reference to the religious authorities as "the Pharisees" (9:13, 15, 16) and "the Jews" (9:18, 22). During Jesus' life and ministry, the Pharisees were only one of many Jewish groups on the landscape of first-century Judaism, but this party alone survived the catastrophe of 70 CE. Their rabbinic heirs managed to lead the Jewish people to reconsolidation and recovery, and were the authorities with whom Johannine Christians found themselves in conflict. John 9 thus needs to be read on two historical levels, for in it a story about the life of Jesus is told in such a way that it also reflects difficulties faced by John's early Christian community. Those difficulties may well have included grievous betrayal by family members. "Who sinned, this man or his parents?" was the question with which the story began. Perhaps one answer begins to suggest itself as we ponder the painful disloyalty of the man's own parents.

Another takes shape in the final stage of the investigation, as the formerly blind man is summoned once again before the religious authorities at his parents' behest. In this final round of the investigation, he comes into his own as an adept theologian and sharp-witted interlocutor. The religious authorities reveal their true colors as well, and the lengths to which they are willing to go to deny what is right before their eyes. Indeed, John provides masterful portrayals of "increasing insight" and "hardening blindness."[11]

Initially divided in opinion, the authorities have now closed ranks and place the man under oath to tell the truth, pressuring him to acquiesce to their foregone conclusion: "Give glory to God! We know that this man is a sinner" (9:24). The words "we know" are a red flag in John, signaling spiritual danger (e.g., Nicodemus in 3:2, who first utters them).[12] Yet repeatedly the religious authorities confidently assert what they "know" (9:24, 29) in contrast to the formerly blind man, who disavows theological aptitude, but will not deny his own experience: "I do not know whether he is a sinner. One thing I do know, that though I was blind, now I see" (9:25; see also 9:12).

Moreover, the man is not ruled by his parents' fear, for when asked to recount the healing yet a third time, the religious authorities find themselves on the receiving end of an exasperated question followed by a mocking question: "I have told you already, and you would not listen. Why do you want to hear it again? Do you also want to become his disciples?" (9:27). This witty rejoinder provides the first sign that he may be beginning to think of himself as Jesus' disciple, and it evokes their contempt both for him and for Jesus: "You are his disciple, but we are disciples of Moses" (9:28). They mistakenly presume that following Moses and following Jesus are mutually exclusive options, when they are not. Indeed, in his first open conflict with "the Jews," Jesus invoked Moses as a witness in his own behalf: "your accuser is Moses, on whom you have set your hope. If you believed Moses, you would believe me, for he wrote about me" (5:45–46). Their contempt for Jesus also finds expression in what they take to be a final, insulting comparison: "We know that God has spoken to Moses, but as for this man, we do not know where he comes from" (9:29). The irony of their insult could not be sharper: God spoke to Moses, to be sure, but Jesus is the very incarnation of the Word of God!

At this, the formerly blind man rises to the occasion to address the matter of Jesus' origin, realizing that he can argue theology with the experts after all.[13] They have forced him to think through the theological implications of his experience,[14] and thus he shifts from defensive to offensive mode, making a compelling case for a quite different conclusion. First, he boomerangs the authorities with their own logic, granting them their premise: "God does not listen to sinners," but "does listen to one who worships him and obeys his will" (9:31). He moves from there to another indisputable fact, appealing to another aspect of their shared religious heritage: "Never since the world began has it been heard that anyone opened the eyes of a person born blind" (9:32). So putting two and two together, he reasons, where do you think he is from? "If this man were not from God, he could do nothing" (9:33). In turning the tables on the authorities, asking his own questions of them and defending his healer with such daring, eloquence, and skill, the man once again functions as an *alter Christus*, reflecting the manner in which Jesus will defend himself during his own official trials (John 18–19).[15]

It is the last straw for religious authorities, being lectured on theology by a nobody. Who does he think he is? And doesn't he know who they are? But they cannot refute his logic, and thus they resort to personal attack.[16] Though earlier they denied his blindness in order to dismiss the miracle, now, like the disciples at the beginning of the story, they take it as evidence of sin and make it grounds for refusing to listen to him: "You were born entirely in sins, and are you trying to teach us?" With this, the fate the parents feared devolves upon their son: "and they drove him out" (9:34).

The story thus comes full circle, as the formerly blind man, dubbed a sinner, finds himself on the outside once again. Moreover, Jesus, hearing that they had driven him out, reenters the narrative, again taking the initiative to engage him. Having granted physical sight in their first encounter, he now invites the man to take one step further into full spiritual sight as well: "Do you believe in the Son of Man?" (9:35). It is a step the man is willing and eager to take: "And who is he, sir? Tell me, so that I may believe in him" (9:36). When Jesus identifies himself as the Son of Man, the one who makes God known, the man responds immediately with full confession and devotion: "'Lord, I believe.' And he worshiped him" (9:38). It is the conclusion of a long journey from outer sight to inner insight. The man has moved from his initial perception of Jesus as one who healed him (9:11), to dawning recognition of him as a prophet (9:17), then as one who must have come from God (9:33), and finally as Lord (9:38). In worshiping Jesus, the man acknowledges the very presence of God in him (4:20–24; 12:20), ironically fulfilling the authorities' demand that he "give glory to God" (9:24).[17]

The authorities themselves, however, have failed to do so, for one gives no glory to God by dishonoring God's Son, and thus they are held accountable as the chapter comes to a close: "I came into this world for judgment so that those who do not see may see, and those who do see may become blind" (9:39). Some of the Pharisees, overhearing this, can hardly believe that Jesus could be speaking of them: "'Surely we are not blind, are we?' Jesus said to them, 'If you were blind, you would not have sin. But now that you say, "We see," your sin remains'" (9:40–41). Here, at last, is a decisive answer to the question "Who sinned?"—one that reverses earlier verdicts. Sin has nothing to do with being born blind (9:2, 34), or violating the law (9:16, 24, 29), but rather with resistance to Jesus, with refusing to see when the light of the world and the works of God in him are right before one.[18] Indeed, light produces blindness as well as sight, for those who stare at it and refuse to recognize its power can be blinded. In the final analysis, sin and the true state of one's vision are determined by whether one recognizes the revelation of the works of God in Jesus.

This distinctive understanding of sin needs to be appreciated on its own terms. As Gail R. O'Day astutely points out, the Fourth Gospel "reduces sin to its christological, and hence *theological,* essence. Sin is fundamentally about one's relationship with God, and for the Fourth Evangelist, the decisive measure of one's relationship with God is one's faith in Jesus. This flies in the face of views that want to define sin in relation to right actions and thereby establish the norms for judgment."[19] What this means is that it is not our responsibility, as it was not the Pharisees', to judge anyone's sins: "determination of sin rests with God and Jesus, . . . and is determined by faith, not actions. The Johannine Gospel is thus the most radical example of salvation by grace in the NT."[20] Moreover, this distinctive understanding of sin has implications for an understanding of salvation: "The Fourth Gospel quite explicitly relocates the offer of salvation to Jesus' life and moves away from a narrow focus on Jesus' death. The Gospel is unequivocally clear: Jesus' incarnation, not the expiation of his death, brings salvation from sin."[21] In all of these ways, the Fourth Gospel stretches the horizon of our vision. It is not the only perspective on sin and salvation in the New Testament, but represents a unique and important contribution to Christian theological reflection.

John 9 thus presents the obdurate Pharisees as a paradigm of sin and concludes on a very harsh note, but harsh words are part and parcel of polemics, and we need to bear in mind that New Testament portraits of the Pharisees are caricatures, deeply colored by polemics. As Craig Keener reminds us, "The arrogance of many Pharisees in this Gospel does not fit what we know of Pharisaic or rabbinic ethics."[22] But the Pharisees, or more precisely, their post-70 rabbinic descendants, were the religious authorities with whom John's community found itself in conflict, and it is important to bear in mind the significance of this two-level story for the dislocated community to which it was first addressed. Like the man born blind, members of this community had found their eyes opened by the light of the world, and like him they had suffered expulsion from the synagogue for their confession of faith. They knew what it was to be doubted by neighbors, abandoned by families, questioned, insulted, and cast out. But kicked out the door of the synagogue by their religious leaders, sorry shepherds, they too were found by one who said "I am the door" (10:7), "I am the good shepherd" (10:14), and "anyone who comes to me I will never drive away" (6:37). Indeed, the Good Shepherd Discourse follows directly on the heels of John 9 in John 10 and represents a continuation of it. Therefore, we should not let the idyllic sheep talk fool us, for polemics continue to lie just below the surface of it. Sorry shepherds fall under harsh condemnation, and those whom they have betrayed are assured of another door through which to enter, of a new flock to which to belong, and of a faithful shepherd who knows them by name, leads them out, and lays down his own life for his sheep.

CONNECTIONS

Traditionally, John 9 has been part of the church's reflection during its journey through Lent, a season of self-examination, and appropriately so as it invites us to examine the state of our vision. The story includes a wide cast of characters, and thus many seats that we might occupy. So with whom do we most identify? Those to whom John 9 was first addressed saw their own story embodied in the experience of the blind man. But we should not too quickly limit our reflection, assuming that our only point of identification is with him as well. As we had occasion to note when examining Nicodemus's story in John 3, those of us who are sincere, learned, religious folk perhaps ought to consider our affinities with the religious authorities in this story. Nicodemus, after all, was one of their number, and we may recognize in him and his colleagues our own tendencies to "too readily presume" that we "understand the Christian mystery," "to be overly confident in our faith-based religious knowledge . . . so that we are not prepared to hear what is really new in the revelation of Jesus."[23] We too might find ourselves resisting "the challenge of ongoing revelation,"[24] for in John 9, as in John 3, it appears that what we think "we know" can get in the way of what we see, especially if we consider our own illumination sufficient.

In fairness to the Pharisees, there is a logic to their position. Raymond Brown points out that it probably goes like this: "God commanded that the Sabbath be kept holy; our ancestors decided that kneading clay was menial work that violated the Sabbath; Jesus kneaded clay on the Sabbath, and so he violated God's commandment."[25] However, Brown also astutely notes:

> The difficulty with such reasoning is the failure to recognize that all such interpretations of God's will, no matter how well intentioned, are phrased in our earthly language and thus conditioned. Those positions

we regard as definitive tradition are *true, but in regard to the issues that were in mind when they were formulated.* The Hebrews as slaves in Egypt had to work with clay to make bricks for the Pharaoh, and so kneading clay would justly be classified as servile work forbidden on the Sabbath. But the people who made that classification scarcely thought of kneading a scrap of clay to open a blind man's eyes.[26]

In short, "As one who has come from God, [Jesus] challenges our earthly perceptions of God at any time and cautions us about applying religious judgments from the past, without nuance, to *new* situations."[27] This caution is pertinent in every age, as the church engages in ongoing discernment of the will and work of God in new times and places.

Perhaps we ought also to reflect on affinities we might have with the disciples, the neighbors, or the parents who also occupy the stage in John 9. Like the disciples, do we assume a link between misfortune and sin, and find ourselves asking questions like, "What did they do to deserve this?" And is this abstract theological speculation, this moralizing, ever a means by which we evade commitment and action to relieve human suffering? Or like the neighbors, have we paid so little attention to the destitute in our midst that we scarcely recognize them, and speak *about* them rather than directly *with* them of their circumstances? Maybe we too have encountered those whose lives have been so transformed by the work of God in Jesus Christ that they bear little resemblance to their former selves. The parents' perfidy should also elicit sober reflection on our parts. Does fear ever prevent us, too, from standing with those facing difficult ordeals, even members of our own families? Do we know more about the work of God in Jesus Christ than we are willing to let on in public, particularly if it might have consequences for our reputation or job or safety?[28] Maybe we are among the large company of the baptized who nominally accept Jesus, but are not willing to confess him if it costs anything.[29]

That being said, the formerly blind man, in particular, invites our identification and reflection. His very anonymity summons our participation in the story, for there is a sense in which he represents us all. As Sandra Schneiders observes, his is the only case of congenital blindness among the Gospel miracle stories and is "symbolic of the universal congenital incapacity for divine life."[30] In other words, we are all born blind, and if our eyes have been opened it is because we too have encountered the grace and power of God in Jesus Christ, the light of the world—one who illumines for us the meaning and purpose of human life, changing the way we see ourselves and the world around us. New sight may even have brought us, too, into conflict with perplexed neighbors, family, or powers that be, at a cost to our well-being. Perhaps one could even say that every believer, having been identified with Jesus in baptism, is Jesus' surrogate, an *alter Christus* in this world like the man born blind, bearing his witness and engaging his opponents. Archbishop of Canterbury Rowan Williams suggests as much when he articulates Christian identity as follows:

> It can be put most forcefully, even shockingly, if we say that Christians identify themselves not only as servants of the anointed king but as Christ. Their place in the world is his place. By allowing themselves to be caught up into his witness and doing what his authority makes possible for them, in work and worship, they stand where he stands. . . . By living in that place, we come in some degree to share his identity, to bear his name and to be in the same relationships he has with God and the world.[31]

As we reflect further on intersections between the experience of the man born blind and our own experience, two aspects of it deserve special attention. One is the role his experience plays in his journey to inner sight. Various people try to interpret it for him and to determine appropriate labels that apply; but throughout his interaction with them, he considers himself competent to judge and testify about his own experience, for he knows what has happened to him: "One thing I do know, that though I was blind, now I see" (9:25). Moreover, that experience becomes a lens through which he thinks about the implications of his encounter with Jesus Christ.

Not too long ago, I encountered someone with a strong bond of connection to the man in John 9: a seminarian of unusual gifts and graces, one of the finest candidates for ordained ministry I have known. But he has recently figured something out about himself: he is gay. It was an experience of God's grace in his life that opened his eyes—one that liberated him and allowed him to see himself as he really was—indeed, as God created him to be. But new sight came with a cost, for what do you do when you are a candidate for ordination, facing a series of interrogations by candidacy committees and ordaining bodies before finally accepting a call? Is it any wonder that he felt a strong bond of kinship with the man in John 9 and his ordeals? Some will no doubt label this seminarian a sinner, even an "abomination." But "one thing I know," he says: "I once was blind, but now I see."

David Rensberger's commentary on the blind man's story struck a chord with him, alerting him to the profound intersection between his own story and John 9. Rensberger observes:

The blind man sets the one thing he is certain of, his own experience, against the standards with which the Pharisees confront him. If it comes down to a clash between what has happened to him and what, according to the rules, can or cannot possibly happen, he has no choice but to assent to the reality he now knows. The blind man's God does not live in a book, not even the book of the law itself, but in the act of mercy that has been done to him. He is not about to give up this act, or the freedom of his God to commit it, even for the sake of Moses. . . . The blind man's understanding of who Jesus is emerges from his struggle with those who would invalidate the experience of his own life.[32]

Others, too, will no doubt find that this commentary resonates with their own experience. In my own first reading of it, "feminist" Christians immediately came to mind, for they too have paid a price for thinking through the implications of God's grace in Christ through the lens of women's experience. They have frequently been castigated for this endeavor, chastised for "bias" and "subjectivity" by those completely unaware of the indispensable role experience plays in their own theological reflection, and falsely accused of abandoning "norms" of revelation such as the Bible. They too have found themselves in conflict with religious authorities and deemed "sinners," "heretical," and a dangerous threat in the life of the church. Taking one's experience seriously as an important component of theological reflection can land one in hot water, as gay Christians and feminist Christians, to mention but two examples, can attest.

But a second aspect of the blind man's experience is worth noting in this connection. Rensberger highlights it when he observes that the man's understanding emerges from his *struggle:*

What is especially significant about the blind man's progressive christological enlightenment is the circumstances under which it develops. He reaches deeper understanding, not in a reflective encounter with Jesus . . . but in the process of *confrontation* with the Pharisees. . . . The blind man's understanding of who Jesus is emerges from his struggle with those who would invalidate the experience of his own life. And this is the model that John holds up to his community: let what has happened to you bring you into conflict with the rulers, with Moses himself if need be; for in this *process* your enlightenment will be completed, and at its end you will meet the one who granted you your sight and know him for who he is.[33]

Indeed, this story "tells us that, for the Johannine community, the truth about Jesus came, not at the beginning, nor even simply at the end, but out of the midst of this process of confession, rebuke, and stubbornly continued confession itself." By means of it, they were urged to follow the blind man's example and assured that "even expulsion from the synagogue would mean, not catastrophe, but a deepened encounter with the one who had given them sight."[34]

It is a point worth pondering, because struggle, confrontation, and conflict are realities most of us like to avoid. Is it possible that they could bring us, too, to deepened insight, deepened faith, and deepened encounter with the one who gave us sight? And are not those with whom we sometimes find ourselves in the most intense conflicts members of our own religious communities? No enemy is as dangerous as the enemy within, and "family quarrels" can be the most painful conflicts. It is important to recognize that the conflict in John 9 reflects a family quarrel, as Jews and Jewish Christians found themselves in a difficult process of self-differentiation. Moreover, as Gail O'Day points out, "the gospel's language here reflects an intra-Jewish struggle, and . . . with the complete separation of church and synagogue . . . the context in which this language made any sense ended." Thus, "For the twenty-first-century church, the closest analogy to the situation of the Johannine community is one of intra-Christian struggle, in which one segment of the Christian community finds itself in conflict with the prevailing views of the religious authorities."[35]

Struggle, confrontation, and conflict are inescapable in the life of the church as believers, guided by Scripture, seek to discern and embody the will of God and the implications of the gospel in changing times and places. That discernment is not easy, and requires engagement with often varied, even conflicting, interpretations of Scripture and, consequently, differing conclusions about what God is calling us to be and do. Thus, strange as it may seem, the church has often done some of its best theological reflection in the midst of conflict, which has often proved to be the arena of God's creativity. The distinguished theologian Karl Barth even argued that we should not spare ourselves "relative conflict." John Burgess draws on Barth, along with a sixteenth-century confessional document in the Reformed tradition, to explain: "Only as we grapple with each other's readings of Scripture will we discern what form Christ is taking among us here and now. The Second Helvetic Confession makes a similar point. God can use conflict 'to the glory of his name, to illustrate the truth, and in order that those who are in the right might be manifest.' Relative conflict may be necessary, if the community is finally to determine which readings of Scripture are faithful."[36]

The same can be every bit as true in the lives of individual believers as it is for the community of faith: often, it is by moving through struggle, confrontation, and conflict that we grow in faith, insight, and understanding, as we bring our own experience and theological reflection into conversation—difficult though it may be—with the experience and reflection of others, and thereby find our own conclusions challenged, corrected, rearticulated, sharpened, or refined. The blind man's vision kept improving as he braved his own ordeals, and so, by God's grace, may it be for us, as we too strive to grow more fully into all that God created us to be.

One final point of connection will present itself for a number of people who encounter John 9: those who live daily with disabilities such as blindness. The Gospels are filled with healing stories in which the deaf, the mute, the blind, the paralyzed, the demonically possessed, and the chronically ill are restored to physical health. What must it be like for those who live with disabilities (54 million Americans, for example—one out of six persons—and 600 million worldwide) to hear these stories read in worship and expounded upon in preaching? Far too often, these texts have been hazardous for their health and well-being, subtly (and sometimes not so subtly) conveying fallacies about persons with disabilities. Often, for example, interpretation of them communicates that disabled people need to be fixed, that they are not "whole." Or, since many healing stories in the Gospels emphasize the faith of the person healed, it may be implied that those who are not healed do not have enough faith. More perniciously, interpretation of such texts—even the texts themselves—often establish in the minds of many a clear link between disability and sin. In some instances, for example, texts and interpretations of them convey that disability is a sign of moral imperfection or divine retribution for sin.[37] (Indeed, the disciples and the Pharisees in John 9 assume such a link; see also, for example, 5:14; Luke 5:23.) In other instances, as Kathy Black observes, "Metaphorical interpretations of disability identify the disability of a few with the sins of many: for example, 'We are all *deaf* to the word of God'"[38]—or in the case of John 9, "we are all born *blind*." Disabled persons thereby become symbols of general human brokenness. In short, interpretive hazards abound.

Given the problems such texts and interpretations of them present for the lives and well-being of disabled persons, it is worth noting that the story in John 9 also presents possibilities that can enhance their lives and others' perception of them. Indeed, Black suggests that it is one of the most important texts in the Bible for those within the disability community.[39] For one thing, in John 9 Jesus himself does not accept the sin-disability link assumed by his disciples (9:3–4). He refuses to engage in analysis of the man's situation in any such terms. Instead, he refocuses the attention of the disciples on God's healing mission in the world and claims it as their own. Moreover, faith plays no role in the blind man's healing. Indeed, he does not request it; in this instance, the healing is an unconditional gift granted entirely at Jesus' initiative. But perhaps the most promising feature of the text is the striking characterization of the blind man himself. In most stories, we learn very little about the recipients of Jesus' healing ministry, but this man speaks for thirteen verses and takes center stage. Thus, as Colleen Grant points out, John 9 presents us with a well-developed character, a personality with whom we can identify: "Indeed, despite his anonymity, the man born blind comes alive in this healing narrative in a way that few other characters do. He appears not simply as a broken figure in need of compassion and healing but as a person in his own right. We are able to get to know him as a thoughtful, brave, amusing, but above all, ordinary person."[40]

Moreover, his experience exposes realities with which disabled persons often contend. His neighbors' inability to recognize him, for example, suggests that "blindness" was his defining characteristic for them: "The man's insistence that he is the same man they once knew points out the fallacy of this thinking. From his perspective, his disability was never his defining characteristic; he knows himself to be the same person, blind or sighted."[41] Perhaps their failure to address him directly could even be said to reflect the discomfort and avoidance with which many react to disabled persons, as might the Pharisees' questioning of the man's parents. As Kathy Black observes, "Persons who are blind are often treated as children throughout their adult lives. Strangers will talk to the friends or family of a person who is blind, but are uncomfortable directly addressing the person who is blind. This implies that persons who are blind cannot speak for themselves or understand what is going on around them."[42] In one group with whom I studied this text, parents of a blind daughter immediately recognized this reality, noting that they routinely redirected questioners: "Ask her!"[43] Though John 9 attributes a similar parental response to a different motivation, fear of the Jews, it is nonetheless a striking observation and a familiar experience for disabled persons and their families, and thus worth pondering.

Regrettably, another familiar reality is the suspicion with which a blind person's testimony can be greeted in a court of law, for they are not considered qualified "eyewitnesses."[44] Like the Pharisees at the end of the interrogation, many today have a hard time believing that the disabled "have anything to contribute to society, anything to teach those not blind. Teaching and service is too often assumed to be a one-way street: those who are blind are the passive recipients, not the active givers."[45] By raising all such experiences to visibility, John 9 can perhaps help all of us recognize our participation in prejudicial attitudes and behaviors.

In the end, it is important to note that "even more than in Jesus' act of healing, the work of God is evident in the man's role as witness to Jesus," as Colleen Grant observes.[46] The striking reversal at the end of the story is also worth noting, particularly if we take the closing words of Jesus more literally: "It may suggest that those who are sighted and who perceive themselves as the 'normal' able-bodied members of the church (Surely we are not blind, are we?) may be more in need of healing than the so-called 'disabled.' In other words, as long as our primary perception of ourselves is as persons who can see, or hear, or walk, or think rationally over against those who cannot do these things, our sin of stereotyping and exclusion remains."[47] Surely these observations bear on the full inclusion of disabled persons in the life and ministry of the church. Indeed, "for persons with disabilities to participate fully in the church should not be regarded as something extraordinary."[48]

Interestingly, the early church found in the story of the man born blind a symbol of Christian baptism and the powerful new life that it brings. He is healed, after all, as he washes in water, and "enlightenment" was a term by which New Testament authors referred to baptism (e.g., Heb 6:4; 10:32).[49] Thus the story is depicted repeatedly in frescoes in the Roman catacombs as an illustration of the meaning of baptism, and came to accompany the proselyte's journey of preparation for the rite of baptism during the season of Lent. Baptism continues to be the rite through which all believers take their place among the children of God. By God's grace, maybe the story in John 9 of "an ordinary, amusing, intelligent man, caught up in a situation that brings out his independence and courage,"[50] can help all God's people look at disabled brothers and sisters in Christ with new eyes and fully welcome their presence and ministry among us.

QUESTIONS FOR DISCUSSION OR REFLECTION

Do a dramatic reading of John 9. Assign roles to a narrator, to Jesus, to the man born blind, and his parents. Have the rest of the group read collectively the lines of the disciples and the Pharisees/Jews. Following the reading, debrief the roles: What struck you most about the role you were assigned? What struck you about the roles of others? What questions does the story raise for you?

What does the image of Jesus as "the light of the world" mean to you? What memories or impressions does it evoke?

How has the one who identified himself as the light of the world changed your vision of the world around you? How do you see it differently? Has this ever brought you into conflict with others?

Do you think the link between misfortune and sin is still alive and well? Can you think of instances when the question "Who sinned?" has been entertained to make sense of human suffering? Can such abstract theological speculation be a means by which to evade commitment and action to relieve human suffering, in your view?

Discussion of the man born blind focuses on his disability, but rarely on his poverty (9:8). What do economic considerations contribute to your reflection on the story?

What do you think of the notion that the baptized believer is a surrogate for Jesus, an *alter Christus*, whose place in the world is his place?

What do you think of the Fourth Gospel's distinctive understanding of "sin" as unbelief, as resistance to the revelation of the works of God in Jesus Christ? What appeals to you about it?

What does reading John 9 as a two-level story, reflecting both the life of Jesus and that of the community to which it was first addressed, contribute to your understanding of it?

With whom do you most identify in this story, and why?

What do you think of the parents' unusual role in the story? How would you evaluate their response to the religious authorities? Do you find it to be a display of disloyalty and moral cowardice? Why, or why not?

Has fear ever prevented you from standing with those facing difficult ordeals? Have you ever found yourself in circumstances where you knew more about the work of God in Jesus Christ than you were willing to let on in public? How would you account for this fear and evasion?

Where do you discern connections between the man born blind's experience and your own?

How has your own experience with Jesus Christ proved to be a lens through which to think about the implications of who he is and what he represents?

What do you think about the identification of the gay Christian with the man born blind? In your opinion, is the church's struggle of discernment over the full inclusion of gay and lesbian persons one of those points at which we need to exercise Raymond Brown's caution against "applying religious judgments from the past, without nuance, to new situations"? Why, or why not?

Can you think of any other "intra-Christian" struggles that are illumined by reflection on John 9?

Have you, like the man born blind, ever come to deeper insight, faith, and encounter with God through the process of moving through confrontation? Explain.

Can you think of instances in the church's life when conflict has proved to be the arena of God's creativity, out of which emerged something new?

What does the discussion of physical disability contribute to your reflection on John 9 and other healing stories in the Gospels? What realities about the experience of disabled persons does John 9 raise to visibility for you? What contributions can this story make to the church's reflection on the presence and ministry of disabled persons in its midst?

What new insights have emerged from your engagement with, and discussion of, John 9, and why are they important to you?

8

The Gift of Life: Martha, Mary, and Lazarus

John 11:1–53

Throughout his public ministry as recorded in John, Jesus performs various wondrous works. Though fewer in number than those narrated in Matthew, Mark, or Luke, they are more remarkable. The illnesses he cures have afflicted persons longer: 38 years in one case (5:2–9), the longest illness on record in the Gospels; and in another case, blindness even from birth (9:1–7). Jesus works marvels with nature as well: for example, transforming water into vast quantities of choice wine (2:1–11). All told, the works are only seven in number (2:1–11; 4:46–54; 5:1–9; 6:1–15; 6:16–21; 9:1–7; 11:1–53)[1]—few, but forceful! The most dramatic one, however, is saved for last—"the raising of Lazarus" (11:1–53). Like the wondrous works that precede it, it too is a "sign" (2:11; 4:54; 20:30–31): it points beyond itself to truths about God and life that find expression in Jesus. Indeed, John treats this final, most remarkable of Jesus' signs as his most representative one. More than any other, it epitomizes who Jesus is and what he has come to give us: the gift of life.

Ironically, this dramatic demonstration of Jesus' power to give life precipitates his own death, for the story concludes by noting that "from that day on" the religious authorities resolved to kill him (11:53). When Jesus calls Lazarus out of the tomb, he performs the act that will place himself in one. A difference from the other three Gospels can be noted at this point, for in Matthew, Mark, and Luke, the cleansing of the temple (or "temple tantrum") is the event that precipitates Jesus' death

(Mark 11:15–19; Matt. 21:12–17; Luke 19:45–48). But in John's Gospel the cleansing of the temple takes place early in Jesus' ministry (John 2:13–22), and the last straw is the raising of Lazarus.

"LORD, HE WHOM YOU LOVE IS ILL" (11:1–16)

The story draws us into one of the most intimate and heart-wrenching of human situations: a family desperate with worry over the grave illness of one of its members. There may be no doubt that the situation is a serious one, for Lazarus's condition is underlined three times in the first three verses: "Now *a certain man was ill,* Lazarus of Bethany, the village of Mary and her sister Martha. Mary was the one who anointed the Lord with perfume and wiped his feet with her hair; *her brother Lazarus was ill.* So the sisters sent a message to Jesus, 'Lord, *he whom you love is ill*'" (vv. 1–3). Lazarus is sick—really sick! It is also apparent that this family is one for whom Jesus holds a special affection, for this too is emphasized. He has healed strangers on his journey, but now he is faced with the desperate need of dear friends. Given the ties of affection and faith that bind them, one might anticipate that Jesus, when summoned, would rush immediately to the home of his friends. It jars our sensibilities to read verses 5 and 6: "Accordingly, though Jesus loved Martha and her sister and Lazarus, after having heard that Lazarus was ill, he stayed two days longer in the place where he was."

This is hardly the first time in John that Jesus has appeared to speak or act in a peculiar fashion (cf. 2:4–8; 7:1–10). Once again, we are reminded that Jesus' course of action will not be dictated by the agendas of others, even those of dear friends. On the contrary, Jesus indicates that this desperate situation will be an occasion for revelation: "This illness does not lead to death; rather it is for God's glory, so that the Son of God may be glorified through it" (v. 4). No doubt about it, the delay will occasion more glory, for by the time Jesus finally shows himself in Bethany, Lazarus has exchanged his sickbed for a tomb. Only a resurrection will be able to restore him, not healing. This fatal turn of events will also occasion belief, further accounting for the odd delay. Indeed, Jesus declares his readiness to go to his friends only after he discerns that Lazarus has died: "Then Jesus told them plainly, 'Lazarus is dead. For your sake I am glad I was not there, so that you may believe. But let us go to him'" (vv. 14–15).

Those who read closely will detect premonitions of Jesus' own imminent passion and death in the introduction to this story. Even the evangelist, getting ahead of himself, has identified Mary as "the one who anointed the Lord with perfume and wiped his feet with her hair" (v. 2), though that particular act of devotion, which prepares Jesus' body for burial, will not be narrated until the next chapter (12:1–8). Moreover, in indicating that the crisis at hand is one through which the Son of God will be "glorified," Jesus anticipates the cross toward which this wondrous work will propel him—the hour in which his "glory" is fully seen (12:23; 13:31–32; 17:1, 4–5).

Further premonitions of that hour emerge as the disciples express concern over Jesus' announcement that he intends to go to Bethany in Judea, a short distance from Jerusalem ("some two miles away," v. 18): "Rabbi, the Jews were just now trying to stone you, and are you going there again?" (v. 7; see 5:18; 8:59; and 10:31). He will be returning to a place of danger, a fact that Thomas further acknowledges when he says to the other disciples: "Let us also go, that we may die with him" (v. 16). We do not know whether Thomas speaks out of courage or exasperation. But of one thing we may be sure: this story will bring us closer to Jesus' own death.

"I AM THE RESURRECTION AND THE LIFE" (11:17–27)

Although the story is traditionally referred to as "the raising of Lazarus," the description of that event occupies very little space. Indeed, Jesus continues to take his time in reaching Lazarus, stopping for extended conversations with Martha and Mary en route to the tomb. By means of these preliminary conversations, John carefully unfolds the significance of the wondrous act that is about to take place. Thus we too should pause, for we "ought not to arrive at Lazarus's tomb any faster than Jesus does."[2] Martha and Mary are Jesus' primary conversation partners in John 11, and their encounters with him deserve our full attention. (Lazarus himself utters nary a word.)

You have to love these uppity women. Martha is the first to meet Jesus, and the words with which she greets him clearly convey both complaint and confidence:[3] "Lord, if you had been here, my brother would not have died. But even now I know that God will give you whatever you ask of him" (vv. 21–22). She gives expression to reproach, as well as faith—an important reminder that "our faith is not without feelings of anger in times of crisis."[4] Indeed, we can learn much from Martha and Mary about "adult friendship" with Jesus, as church historian Roberta Bondi attests, when she describes what this story has meant for her own evolving understanding of prayer. Prayer is not "about finding peace, or about accepting whatever happens in life, no matter how tragic, as the will of God." It is rather "a sharing of the whole self and an entire life with God."[5] Indeed,

> it is important that in John 11 Jesus gives no sign that he expects Mary and Martha to relate to him as passive, obedient, little children. Martha and Mary are Jesus' *adult friends*. Because they love him, they are not submissive or subservient. They are not in the least afraid of him. They are not sullenly, silently angry with him. They do not accept what has happened as the will of God. They tell him they are angry with him, and why. As for Jesus, Jesus does not simply tolerate these uppity women. He values them. He chooses them for his closest friends. He trusts them in their anger with him, and he trusts them with his life.[6]

In giving voice to her complaint, Martha also evokes a Jewish tradition of faithful prayer: that of lament, which dares to take God by the lapels, as it were, and speak honestly about the pain of human experience. Her complaint is intertwined with her faith in Jesus' power, for she clearly believes that Jesus could have done something about their desperate need had he been there, and that even now God will give him whatever he asks.

Jesus responds with a promise: "Your brother will rise again" (v. 23), which Martha hears as general words of comfort, of the vague sort often addressed to survivors who stand beside a loved one's grave. She replies in kind: "I know that he will rise again in the resurrection on the last day" (v. 24). The future, in her view, holds promise for all believers, who will share in a resurrection of the dead at the end of time. But Jesus offers much more than that, and speaks directly to correct her view: "I am the resurrection and the life. Those who believe in me, even though they die, will live, and everyone who lives and believes in me will never die" (vv. 25–26).

These words bring us to the theological heart of this story—indeed, to the heart of John's whole Gospel. Jesus is the resurrection and the life, the one who brings fullness of life in relationship with God, both now and in the future. Both present and future are addressed. On the one hand, "those who believe in me, even though they die, will live"—

believers who die will continue to live through resurrection. Jesus affirms that future promise. But, on the other hand, "everyone who lives and believes in me will never die"—that is, believers have eternal life now, long before they reach the funeral home or the end of time. In the present, in the midst of everyday reality, a rich quality of life is experienced in relationship with God, simply by believing in Jesus. It is just as Jesus had said earlier, "I came that they may have life, and have it abundantly" (10:10). Death, then, is but a transition that does not break the bond between the believer and God.

It is important to try to wrap one's head around this point, for it is one of John's most distinctive and important theological emphases. When the evangelist John speaks of eternal life (as he does frequently), he speaks not simply of future hope or of life that lasts forever. He speaks of a *quality* of life that begins now and continues forever, life that partakes of the goodness and joy of God and is full, rich, and enduring. That quality of life emerges from the transforming and fulfilling experience of intimate relationship with God, and is to John's way of thinking fully accessible *now* through Jesus.[7] Indeed, fullness of life in the *present* receives far greater emphasis in John than future hope, though both are affirmed, and may partly explain why Jesus spends so much time with Martha and Mary, the sisters of the deceased, en route to Lazarus's tomb: the Gospel of John's decided focus is on the *living*.

How regrettable, then, that the words "I am the resurrection and the life" are usually reserved just for funerals, where only half of Jesus' promise is heard.[8] Jesus does offer life beyond death in relationship with God, but also more: fullness of life in the present! Thus his offer needs also to be heard in the midst of everyday life. Indeed, it "needs to be repeated to all those whose present is barren, but who try to survive on a distant hope."[9] Surely all of us share a hope for fullness of life on both sides of the grave, a hope expressed succinctly by Henry David Thoreau when he said that he wished to learn now what life had to teach, "and not, when I came to die, discover that I had not lived."[10]

Having declared himself plainly to Martha as "the resurrection and the life"—present and future—Jesus asks an exceedingly important question (important for Martha and for all of us): "Do you believe this?" (v. 26). Martha responds: "Yes, Lord, I believe that you are the Messiah, the Son of God, the one coming into the world" (v. 27). It is the most complete confession of faith heard yet in John's story, on a par with the great confession of Peter in the other Gospels (see Mark 8:29; Matt. 16:16; Luke 9:20). Significantly, that confession appears in John on the lips of a female disciple. Still, one senses that Martha has not fully grasped the import of Jesus' words. In this respect, she represents "faith's growing edge," reminding us that "faith can never be stagnant, for it will always be stretched beyond its own limits."[11] Shortly, Jesus will stretch maturing faith with a radical demonstration of his claim, so that there may be no doubt about his power to give life.

"LAZARUS, COME OUT!" (11:28–53)

Still, Jesus appears in no great hurry to reach Lazarus's tomb, for next he pauses for conversation with Mary. Interestingly, she greets Jesus with the very same words of reproach and faith as did her sister Martha. However, two things distinguish Mary's encounter with Jesus. For one thing, she is accompanied by Jews who have joined her in mourning, offering emotional support in her time of grief. Thus a crowd is on hand to witness Jesus' last sign, and the encounter is now a public one. The second and most intriguing thing about the scene, however, is the intense display of emotion on the part of Jesus: "When Jesus saw her weeping, and the Jews who came with her also weeping, he was greatly disturbed in spirit and deeply moved" (v. 33). Indeed, "Jesus began to weep" (v. 35). He is then described as "again greatly disturbed" when he approaches Lazarus's tomb (v. 38). These references are unusual in a Gospel that places far more emphasis on Jesus' divinity than his humanity. Nowhere else in John is such depth of feeling attributed to Jesus. However, many English translations do not do justice to the language of this text, softening and sentimentalizing Greek verbs (*embrimaomai* and *tarassō*) that quite clearly convey feelings of anger, agitation, and indignation. What, then, is Jesus angry, agitated, and indignant about as he encounters Mary and approaches Lazarus's tomb?

The interpretive possibilities are many. The Jews on the scene offer one interpretation of Jesus' emotional response. They said, "See how he loved him!" (v. 36). However, "the Jews" in John's story are rarely presented as accurate interpreters of events at hand (see 12:27–29). Other possibilities suggest themselves: perhaps he is angry at Mary and Martha's unbelief (as some commentators maintain); or, alternatively, angry at the destructive power of death in the world and the way it disfigures human existence. It is also possible that this scene is John's Gethsemane, for only here in John is it said that Jesus is troubled and disturbed in spirit—as well he might be, for his raising of Lazarus will precipitate his own death.

Whatever the case may be, finally, Jesus stands before the tomb (though it has taken 38 verses to get there). But two further interruptions forestall immediate action. First, though he gives the order, "Take away the stone" (v. 39), Martha reappears and seeks to prevent him: "Lord, already there is a stench because he has been dead four days" (v. 40). In so doing, she underlines the stark reality of death before them. Popular belief held that the soul of the deceased hovered near the grave for three days.[12] That Lazarus has been dead four days (noted also in 11:17) confirms that he is dead as a doornail, as does the stench of death's decay. Jesus, however, insists on proceeding, affirming once again that the events at hand will occasion both revelation and belief. But then he himself delays the action further by pausing to pray. In so doing, he directs the attention of the gathered crowd to the God who acts in and through him, leaving no doubt as to the source of the power by which he will raise Lazarus from death.

Then, at long last, "he cried with a loud voice, 'Lazarus, come out!' The dead man came out, his hands and feet bound with strips of cloth, and his face wrapped in a cloth. Jesus said to them, 'Unbind him, and let him go'" (vv. 43–44). The one who "calls his own sheep by name and leads them out" (10:3) summons Lazarus from the tomb. The careful description of the grave clothes in which Lazarus is bound anticipates the close attention to Jesus' own grave clothes in 20:6–7, which, by contrast, are left behind when Jesus emerges from the tomb. At the heart of the scene, however, is the astonishing reality that "the dead man" lives! If actions speak louder than words, Jesus could have provided no more radical demonstration of his power to give life—both in the present, on this earth, and as a promise that on the last day he will raise the dead.

The aftermath of this sign in verses 45–53 suggests that the world finds Jesus' power to give life a threatening thing, for "from that day on they planned to put him to death" (v. 53). So radical is this sign that a plot to kill Lazarus will soon also unfold (see 12:9–11), in hopes of eliminating the walking testimony to the gift of life, as well as its giver. Another death and resurrection is on the near horizon, for which we are now prepared. We have stood in the presence of a tomb, a stone, and grave clothes. We have heard weeping, the question "Where have you laid him?," prayer, and a loud cry. As Fred Craddock observes, "It is as though one held up to the light a sheet of paper on which was written the story of the raising of Lazarus. But bleeding through from the reverse side of the paper, and clear enough to be read, is the other story of the death and resurrection of Jesus."[13]

POSTSCRIPT

In recent years, the story in John 11 has begun to raise new questions about the historical circumstances of the community to which the Gospel of John was first addressed. This Gospel, more than any other, bears signs of stress and conflict, and it is widely assumed that members of the Johannine community suffered expulsion from the synagogue for their confession of faith in Jesus Christ. Only in John does the Greek word *aposynagōgos*, meaning "one who is put out of the synagogue," appear (three times, in 9:22; 12:42; 16:2). The story of the man born blind (John 9), who suffers this fate, has come to be regarded as the key that cracked the puzzle, a window onto circumstances to which the Gospel was addressed. It has prompted a reading of the Gospel as a whole as a two-level story; that is, a story about the life of Jesus is told in such a way that it also reflects difficulties faced by John's early Christian community. Many scholars have found this "expulsion theory" a compelling one that illumines the Fourth Gospel, particularly its hostile polemic toward "the Jews." Indeed, it is so compelling that we have tended to forget that it is a hypothesis that cannot be proved.

However, cracks in the hypothesis have begun to appear, in large part due to the probing questions of a Jewish New Testament scholar, Adele Reinhartz, who argues that it rests on slim evidence (the three "expulsion" references) and does not take account of all the data the Gospel presents. In her view, the story in John 11, in particular, challenges any view of wholly antagonistic relations between John's community and its Jewish neighbors. In it two grieving sisters openly acknowledge their faith in Jesus as Messiah, yet they are supported in their time of need by "the Jews" (11:30–37, 45). If John 11, like John 9, is to be read as a two-level story, would it not imply a measure of tolerance and acceptance among the Jewish community for those who openly believed in Jesus—women like Martha and Mary, who seem to rely on the Jewish community's emotional support in their time of need?

Reinhartz points out that other texts in John also support a more complex view of relations between the Jewish and Christian communities. In John 12:10–11, for example, the chief priests plan to put Lazarus to death, "since it was on account of him that many of the Jews were deserting and were believing in Jesus." The language of "desertion" (the verb *hypagō* in Greek) implies voluntary departure rather than forcible exclusion. In short, Reinhartz concludes that "a two-level reading of chapter 11 would suggest that Johannine Christians maintained social relationships with the Jewish community and that the Jewish community itself continued at least in part to show some degree of awareness of, interest in, and openness to Jesus."[14]

Reinhartz's reading represents a significant challenge to the traditional expulsion theory and is important in several respects. For one thing, it suggests that the relationship between the Jewish and Christian communities in John's locale may well have been more complex than the standard expulsion reading allows. It also reminds us that we are hearing only one side of the story—the evangelist's perspective on events. Indeed, some now wonder if "expulsion" identifies a historical action or an emotion. As Robert Kysar explains in commenting on the three expulsion texts (9:22; 12:42; 16:2), "The Jewish Christians *may have felt* the leaders of their synagogue had kicked them out of the community. That is really as much as those passages may tell us. The feelings expressed by the Johannine Christians might have been much like some discontent Christians or Jews today who claim that a particular congregation 'drove them out.'"[15]

Most importantly, Reinhartz places an important ethical challenge squarely in the laps of Christian readers and interpreters, where it belongs. The expulsion theory has made it possible for us to "justify" the bitter anti-Jewish rhetoric in John—indeed, to blame it on the Jews, who supposedly evoked it by forcibly evicting Christians from the synagogue. It has given us an excuse to let our Christian forebears off the hook and to avoid struggling with the anti-Judaic features of John that are part of *our* dirty laundry, our Christian heritage. In all of these respects, Reinhartz raises salutary questions that need to inform engagement with the Gospel of John.

QUESTIONS FOR DISCUSSION OR REFLECTION

The story of "the raising of Lazarus" is one of the most dramatic in John and demands a dramatic reading. Assign roles to a narrator, to Jesus, to Martha, to Mary, to Thomas, and to Caiaphas. Have the rest of the group read collectively the lines of the disciples, the Jews, and the religious authorities. Then share briefly: What most captures your attention as you hear the story? What questions does the story raise for you?

What do you make of Thomas's statement in verse 16? Do you imagine that the tone of his voice conveys courage or exasperation?

Had you ever noticed the attention given to Jesus' conversations with Martha and Mary in John 11? In the past, lectionaries have sometimes skipped over these conversations, bringing Jesus more directly to the tomb. What do you think of these omissions? What do these conversations contribute to your reflection on the story?

Do you ever complain to God in prayer? Why, or why not? Would you agree with Roberta Bondi that Martha and Mary have much to teach us about "adult friendship" with Jesus? What do you learn from them?

Do you, or persons you know, find yourselves waiting for *real life* to begin, longing for fullness of life in the midst of a seemingly barren present? What are you, or they, waiting for? What does this story contribute to your reflection in the midst of such reality?

When people speak of "eternal life," to what do you think they most often refer? What does it mean to you? How does this story reframe our understanding of what "eternal life" entails?

There are many "tombs" that can imprison us and deaden our spirits well before the grave. What "tombs" keep you or persons you love from fullness of life in the present?

When Lazarus emerges from the tomb, Jesus directs the friends and family gathered to "unbind him, and let him go" (v. 44). How can we assist in the unbinding of others, that they may experience the fullness of life that is God's gift to us in Christ? How have brothers and sisters in Christ played a role in your own unbinding, enabling you to embrace fullness of life?

When you wake up in the morning, what do you find yourself thinking about first: the past, the present, or the future? Why do you think this is the case? What does John 11 contribute to your reflection on this question?

You may wish to compare different English translations and note the variety of ways that Jesus' emotions are described in verses 33–38. How do you interpret the intensity of Jesus' emotional response in this scene?

What do you make of the close attention to the grave clothes of both Lazarus and Jesus in 11:43–44 and 20:6–7, and the contrast between the two?

Interestingly, Lazarus has no voice of his own in this story. We do not hear him speak. What do you imagine he might have said? Is there anything you would have liked to discuss with him?

With whom do you most identify in this story: Martha, Mary, Jesus, or Lazarus? Why?

Share your reactions to Reinhartz's observations about John 11, her critique of the expulsion theory, and the ethical challenge she represents.

9

The Anointing and Washing of Feet

John 12:1–8 and 13:1–20

Feet figure prominently in two stories at the very center of John's Gospel: those of Jesus, anointed by Mary in chapter 12, and those of the disciples, washed by Jesus in chapter 13. The setting for each story is that of a supper at which members of Jesus' inner circle are present, the only two recorded in John. The first is shared with Martha, Mary, and Lazarus, among others, and anticipates Jesus' burial. The second is Jesus' Last Supper, shared with disciples on the eve of his departure, and anticipates his death. Both stories help us grasp what it means to be a disciple of one who gave of himself fully in love for us, even unto death.

MARY ANOINTS JESUS' FEET (12:1–8)

All four Gospels feature an anointing of Jesus by a woman (Mark 14:3–9 // Matt. 26:6–13; Luke 7:36–50), but each has distinctive features and should be examined on its own terms. (Thus we should resist the impulse to mix and match quite different Gospel narratives.) Only in John is the woman identified by name: Mary, the sister of Lazarus who was raised from the dead. Indeed, in John's Gospel the story of the anointing becomes the sequel to the raising of Lazarus. The formerly "dead man" himself is seated at the table in fellowship with Jesus, and his sister Martha serves them. The proximity of the anointing to the raising of Lazarus suggests that the gesture Mary offers is one of boundless gratitude for bringing her brother back to life: "Mary took a pound of costly perfume made of pure nard, anointed Jesus' feet, and wiped them with her hair. The house was filled with the fragrance of the perfume" (v. 3). This act of devotion is clearly extravagant, underlined by its quantity (a full pound), its cost, and pointed reference to the fact that its fragrance suffused the entire house. It is one of the few smells on record in the New Testament, and contrasts dramatically with the "stench" anticipated by Martha at Lazarus's tomb (11:39). A fragrant smell and grateful love now fill a house that had once been filled with mourning and the smell of death's decay.

The scene brings to mind another in the New Testament in which the sisters Martha and Mary appear (Luke 10:38–42). In both, Martha is "serving" while a devoted Mary is positioned at Jesus' feet. In John's Gospel, however, the two sisters are not contrasted or pitted against each other, as they are in Luke. Instead, the foil for Mary is Judas, who protests her act of devotion: "Why was this perfume not sold for three hundred denarii and the money given to the poor?" (v. 5). One denarius was a full day's wage at the time, so Judas's protest further underlines the fact that Mary's gesture is indeed extravagant, but in his view an extravagant waste.

These are the only words that Judas utters in John's Gospel, and they are undercut by asides from the narrator, both before and after he speaks, identifying him as the Lord's betrayer, and as one who cared not a whit for the poor—in fact, he is a thief (vv. 4, 6). Even so, Judas's protest may strike many of us as appropriate, having considerable merit. As Fred Craddock observes, his question may come to our minds as well when three hundred poinsettias fill the chancel at Christmas and five hundred lilies at Easter.[1] Could not a more worthy cause be found in which to use the funds expended on a fleeting display of devotion? Craddock notes that Mary's act of gratitude is likely both to bless and to plague us: "'a sinful waste,' says not only Judas, but everyone who has seen hollow eyes over a tin cup or heard the whimpering of a hungry child."[2]

Jesus, however, defends Mary in the face of this protest: "'Leave her alone. She bought it so that she might keep it for the day of my burial. You always have the poor with you, but you do not always have me'" (vv. 7–8). It is the first mention of his burial in John—now inevitable in light of the death sentence under which he stands (11:53). His days in their midst are limited, as Mary apparently recognizes, and he accepts and defends her extravagant act of devotion. He acknowledges that

Mary has performed a prophetic act as well as a grateful one in the face of his imminent death by anointing his body for burial. After his crucifixion, Jesus will be anointed for burial again, but in secret by men who are afraid to confess their faith openly (19:38–42). Mary has offered her gesture of devotion in full view of others, while he still lives.[3]

Mary's gift will take on even greater significance as the narrative unfolds. Her self-effacing gesture of anointing Jesus' feet and wiping them with her own hair anticipates a similar humbling gesture on the part of Jesus in chapter 13, when he disrobes, then washes and wipes the feet of his disciples as a sign of his impending death on their behalf. What she has done for him, and he for them, he will instruct his disciples to do for one another. In retrospect we are able to see that Mary has intuitively modeled what it means to be a disciple before instruction in this matter is explicitly given.

JESUS WASHES THE DISCIPLES' FEET (13:1–20)

John's story of Jesus' final meal with his disciples, like the story of the anointing, should be read on its own terms, for it differs in significant respects from accounts of the Last Supper recorded in Matthew, Mark, and Luke. For one thing, John's Last Supper is not a Passover meal (13:1); "Jesus does not *eat* the Passover; he *is* the Passover."[4] As "the Lamb of God who takes away the sin of the world" (1:29), he is handed over for crucifixion at the same hour that the paschal lambs began to be slaughtered (19:13–16, 36). Moreover, we should not necessarily imagine that Jesus shares his final meal with but "twelve" disciples, for that number is not specified. Only rarely does the evangelist refer to "the twelve" (6:67–71 and 20:24). John plays down their role and uses the term "disciples" to describe a much wider group of followers (cf. 6:66).[5] That group clearly included women, and is one in which the evangelist hopes that readers will locate themselves. Finally, and most arresting of all, John's final meal does not feature the institution of the Lord's Supper. There are no parting words of Jesus over bread and wine, no "do this in remembrance of me." Instead, a foot-washing story, found in no other Gospel, stands in its place.

This final meal indicates a critical turning point. Indeed, 13:1 is the hinge on which John's Gospel pivots: "Now before the festival of the Passover, Jesus knew that his hour had come to depart from this world and go to the Father. Having loved his own who were in the world, he loved them to the end." The public ministry of Jesus is over, and Jesus' long-anticipated "hour" is at hand. From this point on, John directs attention to the departure of the Word made flesh, his "lifting up" on the cross, by which he will return to his heavenly Father. Jesus approaches his cross as an expression of his love for his disciples— indeed, the place where his love for them will find its fullest and most visible expression. That same love now compels him to prepare his disciples for his departure with a symbolic act that conveys both the nature of discipleship and the significance of his death.

That act is placed in the context of Jesus' sovereignty, his full awareness and control of the events now unfolding: "during supper Jesus, knowing that the Father had given all things into his hands, and that he had come from God and was going to God, got up from the table, took off his outer robe, and tied a towel around himself. Then he poured water into a basin and began to wash the disciples' feet and to wipe them with the towel that was tied around him" (vv. 3–5). Paradoxically, Jesus chooses to exercise his power with an extraordinary demonstration of love and humility. The washing of feet was an act of hospitality customarily extended to dinner guests to clean the dusty, sandal-shod feet on which they had traveled. A basin of water and a towel were provided for them to wash their own feet, or a slave might be required to perform this menial task. Jesus, however, takes on the role of both host and slave by providing this act of hospitality and performing it himself. Simon Peter, expressing the disciples' embarrassment at this turn of events, sees it as an astonishing breach of social convention and insists that he will not allow it: "You will never wash my feet" (v. 8). What could Jesus' astounding act possibly mean?

Two interpretations of the foot washing are presented in the story: the first asks disciples simply to receive Christ's act of hospitality (vv. 6–11); the second, to extend it to one another (vv. 12–15). Interestingly, the first interpretation is often overlooked, and the second overemphasized in the church's appropriation of the story, perhaps because it is far easier to extend hospitality than to receive it. Apparently, what the foot washing means for the church's understanding of itself "has not really soaked in yet."[6]

The first interpretation of the foot washing emerges in Jesus' exchange with Peter (vv. 6–11) and conveys the understanding that Jesus has performed this symbolic act as a sign of his love for them and of his own humiliating death in their behalf. Jesus compromises his dignity by removing his clothes (which will only again be removed at the cross;

19:23–25) and deigning to wash their feet, like a servant. In fact, the same Greek verb, *tithēmi*, used to describe Jesus' "laying down" of his clothes (13:4), was used earlier to describe the Good Shepherd's "laying down" of his life for his sheep (10:11, 15, 17). Foot washing is an act of extraordinary intimacy. With this profound expression of love in humiliation, performed in anticipation of his death, Jesus draws them into intimate relationship with himself—the same intimate relationship that he enjoys with God. When Peter protests, insisting that he will not allow it, "Jesus answered, 'Unless I wash you, you have no share with me'" (v. 8), that is, no fellowship or abiding relationship. Thus Peter, with typical overexuberance, swings in the other direction, saying, in effect, "since you put it that way, give me a bath!" (v. 9).[7] Peter still misunderstands, however, for it is not the washing that is important, but the death that it symbolizes, as Jesus emphasizes when he insists that only the feet need to be washed (v. 10). In demeaning himself to wash his disciples' feet, Jesus is acting out beforehand his humiliation in death. That death has cleansing power, for the love that draws disciples into intimate relationship with Jesus removes their alienation and estrangement from God.

This first interpretation of the foot washing in verses 6–11 asks disciples and the church simply to *receive* Jesus' expression of love, accepting it fully. This is not always easy to do. As commentator Gail O'Day observes, "The foot washing removes the possibility of distance between Jesus and his followers, and brings them face to face with the love of God for them. Peter's initial responses (vv. 6, 8) and the mention of Judas's betrayal (vv. 2, 11) make clear that accepting this gesture of love and hospitality is indeed a challenge for those who follow Jesus."[8] Many of us find it far more difficult to receive hospitality than to extend it to others, and reflecting on this reality may help us understand something of Peter's resistance, and the church's tendency to bypass this first interpretation of the foot washing. However, learning to receive hospitality is central to our growth in faith, or we may never understand God's love for us in Christ that comes as a gift we did not merit or earn.

It is a crucial dimension of the story, not to be overlooked. Indeed, the interaction between Jesus and Peter graphically portrays a theme writ large throughout Scripture: "the tenacity of human resistance to the self-giving love of God."[9] As Marianne Meye Thompson observes,

> Human beings do not naturally respond either to God's moral commands or to God's saving initiatives; rather, it is precisely in encounter with God's activity that human recalcitrance and resistance disclose

themselves most fully. Apart from God's steadfast faithfulness in seeking and shaping a responsive people, human beings will pursue their own ways, resisting the call to align themselves with God's ways in the world. As this passage so graphically illustrates, human beings instinctively seek to protect their own positions of power and privilege, and they recoil at the thought of power embodied in self-giving and humility.[10]

The second, and far more familiar, interpretation of the foot washing asks disciples and the church to follow Christ's example: "After he had washed their feet, had put on his robe, and had returned to the table, he said to them, 'Do you know what I have done to you? You call me Teacher and Lord—and you are right, for that is what I am. So if I, your Lord and Teacher, have washed your feet, you also ought to wash one another's feet. For I have set you an example, that you also should do as I have done to you'" (vv. 12–15). Jesus offers himself as a model of humility and service that disciples are to emulate.

If we attend to its implications, however, this second interpretation of the foot washing may well be every bit as challenging as the first, for it is more than a call to "humble service." Does it not also call Christians to deep intimacy with one another? Wes Howard-Brook notes that foot washing invites us to break through barriers to intimacy, and learn to accept one another as we are: "Footwashing calls us to reveal a part of ourselves that is usually hidden."[11] Feet, after all, are not always our most attractive feature. Indeed, they "are an apt symbol for the reality of ourselves," for we can do little to change their appearance. We are stuck with crooked toes, corns, calluses, and discolored toenails. Thus "to invite people to look at, to wash, to care for our feet is to invite them to accept us as we are."[12] Such intimacy entails risk, to be sure, for Jesus called us to such intimacy with him and with one another, fully aware that there are betrayers in our midst.

The challenge deepens when we bear in mind that Jesus washed his disciples' feet as a sign of his willingness to lay down his life for them. It was a symbol of his death. Would not following Jesus' example then also entail a willingness on our parts to lay down our lives in love for one another, if need be, as he has done for us? Christians in El Salvador, Malawi, and other parts of the globe have had to face that challenge, and know what it means to risk one's very life for the faith. Surely, as Howard-Brook observes, only communities of genuine intimacy make such risk possible: "To be able to go out into a hostile world in witness to God's love requires the awareness that one is supported in both the sending and the returning."[13]

Stories of feet—those of Jesus, anointed by Mary, and those of the disciples, washed by Jesus on the night before his death—have thus brought us closer to an understanding of Jesus' giving of himself in love for us and the meaning of our own discipleship in obedience to him. Jesus' feet will carry him to a cross, and ours continue to carry us into the world to bear witness to his love. Novelist Frederick Buechner spoke truly when he observed: "Generally speaking, if you want to know who you really are, as distinct from who you like to think you are, keep an eye on where your feet take you."[14]

LIFE TOGETHER IN THE COMMUNITY OF FAITH

John's foot-washing story has much to contribute to our reflection on life together in the community of faith, as we have seen, and a few final thoughts on this matter are worth noting. New Testament scholar Raymond Brown, for instance, draws our attention to striking parallels between foot washing and celebration of the Eucharist (or Lord's Supper) and then raises an intriguing question for our consideration. As we have noted, there is no institution of the Lord's Supper in John's Last Supper scene—only the washing of feet, though similarities may be observed: the foot washing stands at the same place in the meal, is an action symbolic of Jesus' self-giving in death, and is accompanied by a command to repeat it. The question Brown raises is this: "Because it is so sacred, the eucharist has been very divisive in Christian history with almost every aspect having been fought about. Would Christians have argued with each other so fiercely over the washing of feet? Many Christians vie for the privilege of presiding at the eucharist. How many would vie for the 'privilege' of washing another person's dirty feet?"[15]

It is an interesting question to ponder. An answer to that question might seem obvious: of course we would not argue so fiercely over the washing of dirty feet. But on further reflection, maybe we should not be so sure. We might very well find ourselves arguing, perhaps over the question of how often we should wash feet or whether we should sprinkle or immerse them. And who would be allowed to preside over foot washing and practice it? Perhaps some denominations would argue about whether women can wash feet, others over a proposition that only heterosexual Christians be allowed to wash feet. I, for one, am not as confident as I used to be that we would not be arguing about feet.

New Testament scholar Sandra Schneiders draws attention to another intriguing aspect of the story: what it tells us about the distinctive nature of the service that characterizes life in the Christian community. She notes that there are three very different models of serving in our everyday experience. "In the first model service denotes what one person (the server) *must do* for another (the served) because of some right or power that the latter is understood to possess."[16] It is in this sense that slaves serve owners, women (in a patriarchal society) serve men, subjects serve their rulers, and the rich serve the poor. There is "a fundamental condition of inequality between the two persons, and the service rendered expresses and reinforces that condition of inequality."[17]

In the second model, "service denotes what the server *does freely* for the served because of some need perceived in the latter that the former has the power to meet."[18] It is in this sense that parents serve their children, professionals serve their clients, the rich serve the poor, and the strong serve the weak. However, the basis of the service is still inequality: "The server is perceived by him- or herself and by the served as acting, however generously, out of genuine superiority to the other and the service situation lasts only as long as the server remains superior."[19]

The third, quite different, model is that of *friendship*, "the one human relationship based on equality": "If it does not begin between equals it quickly abolishes whatever inequality it discovers or renders the inequality irrelevant."[20] In friendship, "the good of each is truly the other's good and so, in seeking the good of the friend, one's own good is achieved. . . . Domination is totally foreign to friendship because domination arises from, expresses, and reinforces inequality."[21]

Schneiders points out that the third model characterizes Jesus' action on behalf of his disciples. Though he is superior to them as teacher and Lord, the act he performs to symbolize his death is one of menial service, one that abolishes the inequality between them, deliberately reversing their social positions and roles: "By washing his disciples' feet Jesus overcame by love the inequality that existed by nature between himself and those whom he had chosen as friends. He established an intimacy with them that superseded his superiority and signaled their access to everything that he had received from his Father."[22] Moments later Jesus articulates this explicitly, describing his self-gift as an act of friendship: "I do not call you servants any longer . . . I have called you friends" (15:15).

Schneiders also suggests that this may shed light on Peter's adamant resistance to the foot washing. He may realize that "Jesus, by transcending the inequality between himself and his disciples and inaugurating between them the relationship of friendship, is subverting in principle all structures of domination, and therefore the basis for Peter's own exercise of power and authority."[23] Marianne Meye Thompson makes a similar point when she notes that it may be those with power and privilege who are most challenged by Jesus' example.[24] Whatever the case may be, the implications for life together in community are clear: "what definitely distinguishes the community that Jesus calls into existence from the power structures so universal in human society is the love of friendship expressing itself in joyful mutual service for which rank is irrelevant."[25] The community that exists in Jesus' name embodies "a radically new order of human relationships."[26]

The many dimensions of the foot-washing story are profound, and it is likely to take a while for it all to soak in. Could the actual practice of foot washing help us absorb its many implications? Some churches do include foot washing in their liturgy, especially on Maundy Thursday of Holy Week, when it is featured in the lectionary. But for many of us foot washing is not a regular liturgical practice (even though it is a ritual, like the Lord's Supper, that Jesus asked his disciples to repeat). I had an opportunity once to attend a foot washing on Maundy Thursday, but confess I did not go; for one thing, I could not figure out the logistics and what to do with my pantyhose. But Howard-Brook's point was (to be honest) the source of my deeper discomfort: it is an act of extraordinary intimacy.

Several years ago I was with a group of women at a church conference center who debated late into the night the wisdom of planning a foot-washing service for their next monthly Bible study meeting. The clincher came when one woman observed: "If I announce that we are planning a foot-washing ritual for the next meeting, half the women won't show up that night, and the other half will spend the afternoon getting a pedicure." Do you think she is right about that? Interestingly, Howard-Brook recommends that a group not wash one another's feet unless the members are committed to continuing in relationship with one another: "Practicing footwashing in a setting where no real intimacy is expected among participants risks falsifying and trivializing the ritual."[27]

Moreover, in light of Schneiders's observations about the distinctive nature of service embodied by Jesus' foot washing and what it conveys about the irrelevance of rank among Christians, it might be well to rethink one manner in which foot washing is liturgically practiced: members of the clergy are far too often cast in the role of foot washers. There is a problem with this, as N. T. Wright, a clergyman with experience in this role, admits: "It has become a sign of leadership. When Jesus did it, he was doing what normally a slave would do; but when we do it, we're doing what Jesus did. Though . . . it is a deeply intimate and moving thing to do, it is still, rather obviously, the leader of the congregation copying Jesus—and, in a strange way, having his or her own authority and status enhanced by doing so. Somehow we need to get beyond this."[28] Indeed!

But in the end, whatever our liturgical preferences, John's foot-washing story has power to reshape us as a community of faith, however it is engaged. May the gift of the love reflected in this story—a love without limits, a love "to the end"—draw us closer to God in wonder and gratitude, as well as closer to one another. And may it shape us all for service in this world in Jesus' name.

QUESTIONS FOR DISCUSSION OR REFLECTION

Do a dramatic reading of John 12:1–8 and/or 13:1–20. Assign roles to a narrator, to Jesus, to Judas, and to Peter. Following the readings, share briefly: What most captures your attention as you hear the stories? What questions do these stories raise for you?

What smells does your memory associate with experiences of profound gratitude, or of death and burial?

As you consider the story of Mary's anointing of Jesus' feet, with whom do you identify, and why? If you had been present at that dinner table, what would you like to have said in response to Mary, to Judas, or to Jesus?

Jesus' words in 12:8 ("You always have the poor with you, but you do not always have me") have sometimes been used to justify Christian disregard for the poor. Is this appropriate? How would you interpret Jesus' admonition? You may wish to examine a possible allusion in Deuteronomy 15:11 and reflect on its bearing on this question. Gail O'Day suggests that Jesus affirms a "both/and" love, refuting Judas's "either/or" proposition.[29] What do you think?

All four Gospels feature an anointing of Jesus by a woman (Mark

14:3–9 // Matt. 26:6–13; Luke 7:36–50), but each has distinctive features and should be examined on its own terms. Compare these four stories. What key differences do you note among them? How does this inform your reading of John's version of the story?

Do you find it more difficult to extend hospitality or to receive it, and why? What does this contribute to your reflection on the foot-washing story? How does it illumine your understanding of Peter's discomfort?

What barriers to intimacy exist in your experience of Christian community? How might your congregation foster authentic intimacy among its members?

If any in your group have ever participated in a foot-washing ritual, have them share their impressions of the experience. Would you be willing to participate in such a ritual? Why, or why not? In what settings might such a ritual be appropriate in the life of your congregation?

What do you think of Frederick Buechner's observation that "if you want to know who you really are, as distinct from who you like to think you are, keep an eye on where your feet take you"?[30] Think about all the ways you use your feet. What do they say about who you are? How do they give expression to your faith?

How would you respond to Raymond Brown's intriguing question: "Because it is so sacred, the eucharist has been very divisive in Christian history with almost every aspect having been fought about. Would Christians have argued with each other so fiercely over the washing of feet? Many Christians vie for the privilege of presiding at the eucharist. How many would vie for the 'privilege' of washing another person's dirty feet?"[31] What do you think? Would we argue over the washing of dirty feet? Why, or why not? If so, what do you think we would argue about?

What did you think of Sandra Schneiders's discussion of the three different models of serving in everyday experience? What does it contribute to your understanding of the foot-washing scene and life in the Christian community?

Do you think those with power and privilege are most challenged by Jesus' example in the foot washing?

The story of the foot washing in John 13 is the lectionary reading for Maundy Thursday during Holy Week. How does your congregation observe Maundy Thursday?

How has the love and fellowship of your Christian community
enabled you to walk through difficult life experiences?
What new insights have emerged from your discussion and reflection on this story?

10

Farewell Conversations

John 14–17

One of the most unusual features of John's Gospel is this: by the end of chapter 12, the public ministry of Jesus is over. Yet the story of his passion, death, and resurrection does not begin until chapter 18. Between these two points (chaps. 13–17) John shifts into slow motion, pausing so that we may eavesdrop on Jesus' farewell conversations with his disciples at their last supper together on the night before his death. By means of these conversations (13:31–16:33), and of the symbolic act of foot washing (chap. 13) and of prayer (chap. 17), Jesus prepares them for his departure and for life in his absence. When their table talk concludes, they proceed directly to the garden where Jesus will be betrayed and arrested (18:1).

The conversations to which we are privy are thus private and anguished ones between intimate friends who are about to lose the one who is the center of their life together. Fred Craddock captures the scene in a memorable image, likening the disciples to children playing on the floor, who happen to look up and see the parents putting on coats and hats. Their questions are three (and they have not changed): Where are you going? Can we go? Then who is going to stay with us?[1] These concerns are the focus of John's Farewell Discourse: "Little children, I am with you only a little longer" (13:33). "Lord, where are you going? . . . Why can I not follow you now?" (13:36–37). "Do not let your hearts be troubled" (14:1). "I will not leave you orphaned" (14:18).

By means of these farewell conversations, John addresses more directly than any other evangelist, and at great length, the first major crisis of the church: the departure of Jesus.[2] Indeed, those in possession of red-letter Bibles (in which the words of Jesus are printed in red) will notice that there is more red at this point than at any other in the New Testament. Jesus talks nonstop for five chapters. (As noted earlier, "Wordy is the Lamb," and nowhere more so than in John 13–17.) By listening closely, we too are prepared for continued life in this world in Jesus' absence. We are given to understand how the church exists after Easter. Three central emphases of the conversations will be our focus: a new commandment, the promise of the Holy Spirit or Paraclete, and the church's mission in the world.

"A NEW COMMANDMENT: LOVE ONE ANOTHER"

John is distinguished from the other Gospels by an almost total lack of ethical exhortation. Nowhere in John are disciples encouraged to turn the other cheek, walk the other mile, forgive those who trespass against them, give away possessions, or attend to the poor. Only in the farewell conversations does a "commandment" appear, surfacing early and echoing throughout the discourse: "I give you a new commandment, that you love one another. Just as I have loved you, you also should love one another. By this everyone will know that you are my disciples, if you have love for one another" (13:34–35). It is as close as we get to an ethical injunction in John. Mutual love is at the heart of John's vision of the Christian life. Indeed, it is the identifying characteristic of the community that continues to exist in the world in Jesus' name. Such love keeps the spirit of Jesus alive in the world and has evangelistic import, for as long as Christian love is in the world, the world is still encountering Jesus.

On three counts, however, the commandment may initially strike us as odd. First, we may wonder in what sense the commandment can be deemed "new," for a love commandment was, and is, also central to Judaism (cf. Lev. 19:18). But for John the commandment is new in one important respect: it takes Jesus as its model, who gave the fullest possible expression to God's own love by giving his own life on the cross. This point emerges clearly when the love commandment is restated in 15:12–13: "This is my commandment, that you love one another as I have loved you. No one has greater love than this, to lay down one's life for one's friends."

A second question may also give us pause: can love be "commanded"? Not if it were simply a feeling. But the love of which John speaks is more than the warm feeling one has toward another. It is more than that emotion extolled in Hallmark-speak as "the feeling you feel when you feel you're going to feel a feeling you never felt before." Love, in both the Old and New Testaments, is not just something you feel—far more, it is something you do. Love seeks the well-being of others and is expressed in concrete efforts on their behalf. Thus love can be commanded. Love is something we do, redefined by Jesus' own act of self-giving. Love is something we do, regardless of how we feel; thus it may come as a relief to know that we do not have to like everybody—we just have to love them. A wise teacher, Henri Nouwen, observed: "If we wait for a feeling of love before loving, we may never learn to love well. . . . Mostly we *know* what the loving thing to do is. When we 'do' love, even if others are not able to respond with love, we will discover that our feelings catch up with our acts."[3]

The third peculiarity appears by way of contrast when we recall that the other Gospels exhort disciples to love their neighbors (Mark 12:28–34; Matt. 22:34–40; Luke 10:25–28) and even their enemies (see Matt. 5:43–48; Luke 6:27–36). John's Gospel focuses the love commandment on the community of disciples itself. It speaks of in-house love, calling Christians to "love one another." We ought not to assume, however, that this makes John's love commandment easier to follow. Indeed, commentator Gail O'Day wisely cautions against dismissing the ethical seriousness of this commandment: "The history of the church and of individual communities of faith suggests that to love one another may be the most difficult thing Jesus could have asked. There are many circumstances in which it is easier to love one's enemies than it is to love those with whom one lives, works, and worships day after day."[4]

Those who have ever found themselves in the midst of congregational or denominational conflict know how difficult it can be to love fellow believers, for no quarrel is as fierce as the family feud. In the midst of communal conflict, we may find ourselves empathizing with the little girl who was asked by her Sunday school teacher if she wanted to go to heaven, and said: "Not if all these people are going to be there." I take comfort in the fact that Jesus promised that there are many rooms in his Father's house (14:1–4), and must confess that sometimes I pray, "Please, please, please, Jesus, as you prepare the rooms and make the reservations, don't assign me to a room with . . . ." In my own life at least, and perhaps in yours as well, loving other Christians may be the most difficult thing Jesus could have asked us to do. But to love Jesus is to be obedient to his commandment—not simply for our own sake but for the sake of the world, as we will see when we consider the third major focus of the farewell conversations.

"I WILL NOT LEAVE YOU ORPHANED": THE PARACLETE

Jesus' announcement of his imminent departure (13:33) leaves his disciples anxious and distressed. The blow of this announcement, however, is softened by extraordinary words of assurance and promise (cf. 14:1–4, 6). Chief among them are these: "I will not leave you orphaned" (14:18), a promise that refers to the coming of the Paraclete or Holy Spirit. Disciples will not be abandoned or left to fend for themselves. After Jesus' return to God, the Paraclete will be sent in his name and will accompany them in their continued life and mission in this world.

The concept of the Paraclete is John's own and represents the evangelist's reworking and expansion of traditional understandings of the Spirit. By means of it, John speaks of the Spirit more clearly than any other New Testament witness as a *personal* presence—"the ongoing presence of Jesus while he is absent from earth and with the Father in heaven."[5]

Believers experience the personal presence of the Paraclete in varied ways. The word itself defies translation, for it bears multiple meanings, including that of advocate, intercessor, comforter, and proclaimer. The Greek word *paraklētos* (Paraclete) refers to one who is "called (*klētos*) alongside (*para*)," and the Paraclete is called alongside believers in a variety of capacities.

John's teaching about the Paraclete appears in five blocks (14:16–17; 14:25–26; 15:26–27; 16:7–11; and 16:12–15), each of which provides different insights into the Paraclete's role in the lives of believers. The first thing disciples are given to understand is this: "I will ask the Father, and he will give you another Advocate [*paraklētos*] to be with you forever. This is the Spirit of truth, whom the world cannot receive, because it neither sees him nor knows him. You know him, because he abides with you, and he will be in you" (14:16–17). Interestingly, Jesus speaks of God's gift of "*another* Paraclete," for Jesus himself was the first. The Spirit will be to the church the helper, comforter, counselor, and companion that Jesus has been. Indeed, nearly everything said about the

Paraclete has been said elsewhere in the Gospel about Jesus. Only one difference emerges: unlike Jesus, the Paraclete/Spirit will not go away, but will remain with disciples "forever." Jesus, the Word made flesh, lived on this earth in one time and place. The Paraclete dwells within every believer for all times and in all places, and is thus a more intimate and enduring presence.[6]

As the portrait of that enduring presence unfolds in the farewell conversations, the Paraclete's teaching role receives special emphasis: "I have said these things to you while I am still with you. But the Advocate [paraklētos], the Holy Spirit, whom the Father will send in my name, will teach you everything, and remind you of all that I have said to you" (14:25–26). Being a Christian requires an exercise in memory, and it is the function of the Paraclete/Spirit to bring to our remembrance the story of God's Word in the world. The Paraclete teaches nothing other than what Jesus taught, and keeps believers grounded in the tradition of the Word.

However, the Paraclete is a living teacher who unfolds in new circumstances the implications of what Jesus said. The Paraclete "guides" believers "into all the truth," interpreting in relation to each coming generation the contemporary significance of what Jesus has said and done: "I still have many things to say to you, but you cannot bear them now. When the Spirit of truth comes, he will guide you into all the truth; for he will not speak on his own, but will speak whatever he hears, and he will declare to you the things that are to come" (16:12–13). The Paraclete's teaching role in the community of believers is thus both "conserving" and "creative."[7] That teaching role is to pass on the tradition of what Jesus said and did without corruption, yet also to reveal the mind of Christ in new situations.

In this connection, it is perhaps worth noting that congregations and denominations can find themselves wrestling with the tension between that "conserving" and "creative" teaching presence as they seek to discern the mind of Christ together. Believers are not always agreed on the direction in which the Spirit is leading. Thus it is important to note that the gift of the Paraclete/Spirit is a gift to the whole community. When Jesus talks about the gift of the Paraclete/Spirit, all the "yous" are really "ya'lls"—they are plural. The Paraclete is not a private possession; it is given to and known in the community. Thus it is important for believers to stay together in the midst of disagreement as they pursue discernment, because they need one another to discern what God in Christ, through the Spirit, is calling them to be and do. In the midst of communal wrestling with discernment as believers articulate their deepest convictions, they are challenged and corrected, and the Spirit's leading makes itself known.

Finally, the Paraclete/Spirit accompanies believers as they come into conflict with the world—as surely they will, for they can expect the same reception accorded their master (see 15:18–16:4). When they find themselves called upon to defend their faith or to speak truth to those who hold power, the Paraclete/Spirit appears as a witness: "When the Advocate [paraklētos] comes, whom I will send to you from the Father, the Spirit of truth who comes from the Father, he will testify on my behalf. You also are to testify because you have been with me from the beginning" (15:26–27). Consequently, the Christian is no door-mat—no passive victim—in the face of the world's hatred and perse-cution. The Paraclete dwells within, giving voice to truth and empowering unwavering witness. Moreover, the Paraclete/Spirit places the world in proper perspective for believers. This seems to be the point of these enigmatic words: "when he comes, he will prove the world wrong about sin and righteousness and judgment" (see 16:7–11). The world judged Jesus guilty of sin and condemned him to death, but it was wrong. The very experience of the Paraclete in believers' lives is a sign to them that Jesus was vindicated and raised by God, with whom he now abides.

In these many ways the Paraclete fulfills the promise of Jesus, who said, "I will not leave you orphaned" (14:18). The Spirit's presence more than makes up for Jesus' absence: "it is to your advantage that I go away, for if I do not go away, the Advocate [paraklētos] will not come to you; but if I go, I will send him to you" (16:7). After Easter, the Par-aclete/Spirit, the living presence of Christ, abides forever with the church, accompanying, guiding, and empowering its continued life and witness in the world. Moreover, that Spirit is not confined to charismat-ics or apostles, prophets, teachers, or administrators, but is the posses-sion of every believing Christian.[8] No one has second-class status or secondhand faith, for all have direct access to the Paraclete's revelation of God in Christ. The concept of the Paraclete explains a great deal about the Gospel of John's unique theological vision: its radically egal-itarian view of the church and its testimony to the fullness of life avail-able now, in the believer's present experience. It is one of John's most profound contributions to Christian thought, one that summons disci-ples "to believe in a life shaped not by Jesus' absence, but by the unend-ing presence of God."[9]

"IN THE WORLD" BUT NOT "OF THE WORLD": MISSION

John's vision of the Christian life has profound spiritual depths. But spirituality in John is by no means an otherworldly experience or an end in itself. This Gospel is decidedly world-engaged. Indeed, throughout the farewell conversations, Jesus makes clear that though he is departing the world, his disciples are staying and have a mission in the world that is a continuation of his own (see 17:11, 14–15, 18). From John's perspective, the church is decidedly "in the world," but not "of the world" (17:11, 16 RSV)—a witness to the possibility of a different way of living that challenges the world's false values. The world lives under an illusion that relationship with God is unnecessary, that human existence is independent of its Creator.[10] Jesus demonstrated the truth about God, revealing the love of a gracious Creator; and upon his departure the community of believers continues to bear that witness.

This point finds clearest expression in his final prayer (John 17), which brings the farewell conversations to a grand conclusion. The last thing Jesus does to prepare his disciples for his departure is to pray—the longest prayer of Jesus in any of the Gospels. As we eavesdrop on this prayer we hear Jesus pray first for himself as he comes at last to the hour to which his whole ministry has moved (17:1–5); then for his disciples, that they may be protected and upheld in their mission in the world, which is the continuation of his own (17:6–19). Finally, he expands the circle of those for whom he prays, including those who will believe through the preaching of those first disciples (17:20–26); that is, he is praying for us, the church of the future. And chief among his petitions in our behalf is his prayer for our unity, that we "may all be one. As you, Father, are in me and I am in you, may they also be in us, so that the world may believe that you have sent me" (17:21). How is the world to know God, to be challenged? Not only through hearing our witness to the gospel, but by seeing and experiencing the embodied witness of a community united in love of one another.

As we overhear Jesus pray, what may we discern about the unity of his followers, lest it slip from our grasp? For one thing, it is clear that God is its source, for it is to God that Jesus prays; and he speaks of the relationship of oneness and love that exists between them—a unity that is foundational to any unity we claim. Jesus opens up his relationship with God to include us. He incorporates all who believe in him into the relationship of oneness and love that he shares with God, a oneness and love that believers make visible and tangible in this world by their unity with each other.

Note: Jesus does not pray that we may all be the *same*, but that we may all be *one*—that we might love one another despite the differences that may divide us. The power of that kind of witness is clearly captured in poet and writer Kathleen Norris's description of her first visit to a monastery. This is how she articulates her astonishment:

> The person you're quick to label and dismiss as a racist, a homophobe, a queer, an anti-Semite, a misogynist, a bigoted conservative or bleeding-heart liberal is also a person you're committed to live, work, pray, and dine with for the rest of your life. Anyone who knows a monastery well knows that it is no exaggeration to say that you find Al Franken and Rush Limbaugh living next door to each other . . . Barney Frank and Jesse Helms. Not only living together in close quarters, but working, eating, praying, and enjoying (and sometimes enduring) recreation together, every day.[11]

The power of that kind of witness cannot help but claim the attention of our polarized world, for only the divine love could be behind the mystery of it.

It is important for all in the church to bear this in mind whenever we find ourselves in the midst of conflict, for often it is then that the world is watching us most closely, especially when we are engaged in highly publicized debates. To be "one" is not to say that we will be the same, that we will all agree, that there will be no conflict. But as we listen to Jesus pray, we are reminded that the quality of our life together—our ability to make visible the unique relationship that exists by God's grace among us—is our most convincing testimony to the truth and power of the gospel we proclaim.

Moreover, sometimes, in the midst of church conflict, the claim is made that internal discord is diverting believers from the "real" work of ministry, from far more important mission in the world in which they ought to be engaged. From John's perspective, however, the quality of our life together is integral to that larger vocation. Indeed, conflict provides the opportunity to bear witness to the fact that the gospel makes a difference in how we deal with those with whom we disagree—an important witness to make, crucial to our vocation in a world of increasing polarization and violence. As Jesus said, "By this everyone will know that you are my disciples, if you have love for one another" (13:35); and "The glory that you have given me I have given them, so that they may be one, as we are one, I in them and you in me, that they may become completely one, so that the world may know that you have sent me and have loved them even as you have loved me" (17:22–23). It is an astonishing claim: that the "glory" of God, manifest in Jesus, is now transferred to the community of believers! In a very real sense, "the community of believers displays the continuing incarnation" and is now the place where the presence of God is to be found.[12]

For all of these reasons, Jesus' prayer for our unity is the very heart of his prayer on our behalf, and at the heart of our ministry in the world in his name. May it be daily among our prayers as well. And Lord Jesus, keep praying for us too, that we may all be one, embodying in this world the divine love that is your gift to us, so that the world may know that God sent you.

QUESTIONS FOR DISCUSSION OR REFLECTION

Read aloud the following selections from John's Farewell Discourse: John 13:31–35; 14:15–21, 25–27; 15:12–17, 26–27; 16:7–17; 17:1–26. Following the reading, share briefly: What most captures your attention as you consider these readings? What questions do they raise for you?

As noted, love is not something we feel, but something we do, redefined by Jesus' own act of self-giving. Love seeks the well-being of others and is expressed in concrete efforts on their behalf. Share your reactions to this definition of love.

Share your thoughts about Henri Nouwen's observation: "If we wait for a feeling of love before loving, we may never learn to love well. . . . Mostly we *know* what the loving thing to do is. When we 'do' love, even if others are not able to respond with love, we will discover that our feelings catch up with our acts."[13] Have you ever had this experience?

What demonstrations of love are evident among the members of your congregation or denomination?

Would you agree that it may actually be easier to love our enemies than to love those with whom we live, work, and worship? If so, why is this the case?

When you think about controversial issues that have embroiled your congregation or denomination in recent years, what does it mean to you to love fellow believers with whom you deeply, even passionately, disagree? What might loving one another look like in the midst of church conflicts? Where have you seen such love in evidence? How might you foster it?

Which of John's insights into the Paraclete/Spirit's role in our lives most intrigue you, and why? What is their import for our understanding and practice of Christian spirituality?

Share your reactions to the Paraclete/Spirit's teaching presence in our midst as both conserving and creative. Can you think of examples in which you believe that the Holy Spirit has led the church to embrace new insights in understanding and implementing Christ's will for the church?

Has Christian faith brought you or your congregation into conflict with the world? Why or why not? How has the Paraclete/Spirit empowered you to defend your faith and to speak truth to power?

New Testament scholar Raymond Brown notes both a strength and a weakness in John's concept of the Paraclete. Consider his comment and share your reactions to it:

> The thought that there is a living divine teacher in the heart of each believer—a teacher who is the ongoing presence of Jesus, preserving what he taught but interpreting it anew in each generation—is surely one of the greatest contributions made to Christianity by the Fourth Gospel. But the Jesus who sends the Paraclete never tells his followers what is to happen when believers who possess the Paraclete disagree with each other. The Johannine Epistles [1, 2, and 3 John] tell us what frequently happens: they break their *koinōnia* or communion with each other. If the Spirit is the highest and only authority and if each side appeals to him as support for its position, it is nigh impossible (particularly in a dualistic framework where all is either light or darkness) to make concessions and to work out compromises.[14]

Have you ever had the experience of hearing your name lifted up in prayer by fellow Christians? How would you describe your experience of overhearing Jesus pray for us, the church of the future (17:20–26)?

What does the Gospel of John contribute to your understanding of the church's mission in the world?

In what ways have you or your congregation challenged the world's false values?

As we have noted, Jesus does not pray that we may all be the *same*, but that we may all be *one*—that we might love one another despite the differences that divide us. Share your reactions to Kathleen Norris's description of the embodiment of this reality in the life of a monastery. Is this, or can this be, a reality in your church? Why or why not? What obstacles stand in the way of this?

Jesus' prayer in John 17 suggests that ecumenical commitment is essential to the church's mission. What barriers inhibit our witness to the world that Christ's Spirit makes us one?

How and where have you personally experienced unity with other Christians—in local, denominational, or global settings?

What new insights have emerged from your engagement with the farewell conversations and your discussion with one another? What questions linger?

11

Sovereign in Life and Death: Jesus' Passion

John 18–19

All four evangelists tell the story of Jesus' passion, death, and resurrection, but each with a difference. As we compare and contrast their stories, the differences need not trouble us, for together they expand and enrich our reflection on the significance of these events for our lives. As commentator Raymond Brown observes: "All are given to us by the inspiring Spirit, and no one of them exhausts the meaning of Jesus. It is as if one walks around a large diamond to look at it from different angles. A true picture of the whole emerges only because the viewpoints are different."[1] In this chapter, we turn our attention to John's distinctive presentation of Jesus' passion and death.

THE ARREST (18:1–11)

John's presentation of the passion greatly emphasizes the sovereignty of Jesus, who freely lays down his life in love for his friends (15:13). As the Good Shepherd himself has stated: "No one takes [my life] from me, but I lay it down of my own accord" (10:18). Thus he is no victim at the mercy of his enemies. Instead, he is presented as fully in control of the events of his passion. He has himself dispatched Judas into the night during the farewell meal, urging him: "Do quickly what you are going to do" (13:27). Consequently, he is not surprised when Judas arrives in the garden with an arresting party. He comes forward to meet them, "knowing all that was to happen to him" (18:4). Neither has Jesus been prostrate in the dust of that garden, praying that the cup of suffering would pass him by.[2] Instead, hundreds of armed Roman soldiers and temple police fall flat on their faces, powerless before the one who greets them with the divine name: "I AM" (18:4–6). Jesus permits himself to be arrested on the condition that his followers be released (18:8). He will not allow them to defend him and rejects any show of violence, insisting that he must "drink the cup that the Father has given" him (18:10–11).

Only John among the evangelists notes the presence of Roman soldiers at the arrest—quite a lot of them! The Greek word designating the "cohort" or "detachment" of soldiers present (*speira*, 18:3) referred to a Roman army unit of 600 men or a subdivision of 200; and the word used to describe their "officer" (*chiliarchos* in Greek, 18:12) designated a high-ranking military commander generally in charge of 600–1,000 men (*chilioi* = 1,000). Why does John fill the garden with soldiers, implicating Rome in the arrest of Jesus? Perhaps it is a historical detail that only John preserves. Or perhaps the presence of Roman troops alongside the temple police and religious leaders symbolically conveys the whole "world's" opposition to Jesus. Or perhaps their presence prepares the way for the confrontation between Jesus and Pilate, the Roman procurator, an encounter that takes center stage in John's account of the passion. Whatever the case may be, John underscores official Roman interest and involvement throughout the events of Jesus' passion.[3]

THE TRIAL OF JESUS BEFORE PILATE (18:28–19:16A)

Indeed, the most distinctive thing about John's passion narrative, and the centerpiece of it, is the dramatic encounter between Jesus and Pilate. It is preceded by a brief appearance before Annas, the high priest, who asks very general questions about Jesus' disciples and teaching, to which Jesus responds forthrightly (18:12–14, 19–24)—at the very moment that Peter, by contrast, cowers before his questioners, denying Jesus (18:15–18, 25–27). In John there is no account at all of an interrogation of Jesus by the Sanhedrin, as there is in the Synoptic Gospels, perhaps because interrogation by religious authorities is an ongoing reality throughout Jesus' whole ministry (John 7, 8, 10), and those authorities have already judged him and rationalized his death (see 11:45–57).[4] Thus the Roman judicial process before Pilate dominates John's account of Jesus' passion.

The narrative of Jesus' trial before Pilate is far more elaborate in John than in Matthew, Mark, and Luke, where it consists of only three episodes: Jesus' silence before Pilate's questioning, Pilate's offer to release Jesus instead of Barabbas, and then Pilate's deliverance of Jesus for crucifixion at the crowd's insistence. In John's narration of this trial (18:28–19:16), Jesus is hardly silent in the face of interrogation.[5] Moreover, John's dramatic narrative consists of seven episodes and two alternating stage settings: one outside the praetorium where "the Jews" are gathered, and one inside where Jesus is held prisoner. Pilate shuttles back and forth between the two as the episodes unfold. Raymond Brown has helpfully plotted their sequence as follows:[6]

1. *Outside* (xviii 28–32)
   Jews demand death

7. *Outside* (xix 12–16a)
   Jews obtain death

2. *Inside* (xviii 33–38a)
   Pilate questions Jesus about kingship

6. *Inside* (xix 9–11)
   Pilate talks with Jesus about power

3. *Outside* (xviii 38b–40)
   Pilate finds Jesus not guilty; Barabbas choice

5. *Outside* (xix 4–8)
   Pilate finds Jesus not guilty; "Behold the man"

4. *Inside* (xix 1–3)
   Soldiers scourge Jesus

Outside, the Jews make one consistent demand in each of their encounters with Pilate: the death of Jesus, though the nature of their charge against him shifts as they seek the most effective means to secure this end. First, they identify him as a "criminal," literally, an "evildoer" (18:30), but Pilate is not convinced. Eventually the heart of their case against him emerges: "We have a law, and according to that law he ought to die because he has claimed to be the Son of God" (19:7). Finally, they resort to blackmail to force Pilate's hand, implicitly threatening to denounce him to Caesar: "If you release this man, you are no friend of the emperor. Everyone who claims to be a king sets himself against the emperor" (19:12).

Inside, Pilate poses a question that all four evangelists record: "Are you the King of the Jews?" (18:33). But there the similarities end, for the extent of Jesus' response in Matthew, Mark, and Luke is a terse "You say so" (Mark 15:2; Matt. 27:11; Luke 23:3). In John, however, Jesus turns the tables on Pilate, responding with a counterquestion of his own (18:34). Moreover, John's distinctly loquacious Jesus eloquently defends himself against false charges, clarifying the true nature of his kingdom and his sovereignty. Only John among the evangelists takes pains to answer the charge that Jesus claimed to be King of the Jews, providing a magnificent exposition of Jesus' kingship in both negative and positive terms.

First, Jesus is clear about what his kingdom is not, insisting that it "is not from this world." These words specify not the location of his kingdom but rather its source, and thus should not be misconstrued as a rationale for Christian disengagement from the world. The kingdom of which Jesus speaks is decidedly *in* the world and *for* the world (3:16; 17:15–18) and has political implications, but it has its source elsewhere, from above.

Second, Jesus provides a positive description of his kingship, when pressed by Pilate to clarify the matter: "You say that I am a king. For this I was born, and for this I came into the world, to testify to the truth. Everyone who belongs to the truth listens to my voice" (18:37). Jesus thus exercises his kingship by bearing witness to the truth—to all that he has seen (5:19) and heard (8:26) from the Father. He asserts God's claim on the world, challenging the world's pretense of independence from God so that it might be saved from itself. Moreover, as the one who came down from above to make this witness, he himself is the fleshed-out truth about God (14:6). Those who see the fullness of God revealed in Jesus belong to the truth and bear public witness to it by embodying an alternative way in the world, one that eschews violence and armed struggle (18:11, 36). The question that governs the trial scene is whether Pilate will recognize the truth, for it is he and the religious authorities who are truly on trial—not Jesus.

Indeed, this climactic trial scene brings the theme of judgment, so prominent throughout this Gospel, to a dramatic conclusion. As we have had occasion to observe before, judgment is not associated with the end of history and the second coming of the Son of Man as in the other Gospels. John directs attention to the first, all-important coming down of Jesus from heaven before his public career in the incarnation. As the Word made flesh, Jesus is the very revelation of God who makes God known; so whoever sees Jesus has already seen God. Final judgment is thus a present reality, and it is self-judgment, dependent on the attitude of faith or repudiation that people assume toward Jesus (see 3:17–21; 12:44–50).[7] Grammatical ambiguity gives rise to intriguing irony in the concluding scene of the trial when Pilate brings Jesus outside and approaches the judgment seat (19:13). Many translations indicate that Pilate "sat on the judge's bench" (19:13), but this verse could also be understood to convey that Pilate "seated him [Jesus] on the judge's bench." The latter would make eminent sense in John, for how Pilate and the religious authorities judge Jesus will determine how they themselves will be judged.

It is one of many ironies that pervade this story, most of them predicated on the failure of both Pilate and the religious leaders to recognize who Jesus is and the gift of God that he represents. Pilate, for example, asks what may be the most famous question in the New Testament, "What is truth?" (18:38), when the one who is "the way, and the truth, and the life" (14:16) is standing right before him. It is hardly a genuine query on his part, for he does not wait for an answer. Moreover, at the center of the trial (rather than its end), he has Jesus flogged, and the soldiers place a crown of thorns on Jesus' head and dress him in a purple cloak, mocking him as "King of the Jews" (19:1–3), which, in fact, he is. Thus, at the heart of the trial, this bitter burlesque provides dramatic visual confirmation of Jesus' sovereignty. Following this ironic coronation, Pilate then presents Jesus, invested with his royal trappings, before the crowd with yet another famous line: "Behold, the man!" (19:5 RSV, KJV; "Here is the man!" in the NRSV). These much-discussed words may evoke an earlier description of Jesus as the Son of Man who will render final judgment (5:27–28), thereby "undercutting [Pilate's] own authority as judge and ironically revealing the true nature of the trial."[8] Or perhaps they evoke humanity's creation in the image of God (Gen. 1:26–28), in which case the words ironically direct attention to the one who is the true reflection of God: "Look at this man, and you'll see your living, loving, bruised and bleeding God."[9]

The repudiation of Jesus by "his own" (1:11), however, is an especially bitter pill to swallow for this evangelist, and thus the religious authorities are subject to the most painful ironies. For example, in a show of false piety, they do not enter Pilate's headquarters "so as to avoid ritual defilement and to be able to eat the Passover" (18:28), even as they hand over the "Lamb of God who takes away the sin of the world" (1:29). Moreover, they acknowledge that "it is not lawful" for them "to put anyone to death" (18:31)—indeed, their Torah forbids it—even as they insistently seek the death of Jesus. Moreover, when given a choice, they choose Barabbas over Jesus. Barabbas is identified as a *lēstēs* in Greek, which can mean either "bandit/thief" or "insurrectionist." Thus they choose a "thief" (*lēstēs*) who threatens the sheep rather than the Good Shepherd (10:1, 8, 10, 11, 14), and false messianic hopes rather than the true King of the Jews. The sharpest irony of all, however, is saved for last. Though Pilate finally bends before blackmail, he elicits a high price from the religious authorities before meeting their demand: the complete renunciation of their messianic hopes. "Pilate asked them, 'Shall I crucify your King?' The chief priests answered, 'We have no king but the emperor'" (19:15). It is the most devastating moment in the whole Gospel—a moment in which the official representatives of the Jews renounce their covenant with YHWH. Ironically, they do so on "the day of Preparation for the Passover" at "about noon," the very hour in which their priests begin preparation for the feast recalling God's deliverance of the people and celebrating God's covenant with Israel. Indeed, the Passover liturgy affirmed the bedrock of Israel's faith: "We have no king but YHWH";[10] but all dressed up to celebrate this feast, the chief priests now proclaim "we have no king but Caesar." Having elicited this betrayal, "Then [Pilate] handed him over to them to be crucified" (19:16), sentencing to death a man he knew to be innocent (18:38; 19:6). Thus, as commentator Lamar Williamson observes, by the end of the story Pilate loses his credibility as representative of the world's finest judicial system, and the chief priests lose their credibility as representatives of God, the true king of Israel.[11] They have pronounced their own sentences, and the real trial is over.

One last question hovers over the scene, for scholars are divided in the end as to how to interpret John's portrait of Pilate. Is he presented as a "weak" character or a "strong" character? What is one to make of his "shuttle diplomacy," as he goes back and forth between inside and outside settings, between Jesus and the Jews? Some interpreters maintain that this movement robs him of narrative stability and reflects "the struggle taking place within his soul."[12] He is a would-be neutral man, who "will not face the challenge of deciding for Jesus and against 'the Jews'; he thinks he can persuade the Jews to accept a solution that will make it unnecessary for him to decide in favor of Jesus."[13] Indeed, he would "gladly acquit Jesus," but "through lack of resolve and susceptibility to political pressure" he "all too easily becomes the tool of 'the Jews' and their malevolence."[14] He thus represents a reaction to Jesus that is neither faith nor rejection, and illustrates the impossibility of compromise in an encounter with Jesus, the inevitability of decision. What we learn from him is that not to decide is to "inevitably finish in the service of the world."[15]

Others, however, construe Pilate as a "strong" character, who is hostile to the Jews and by no means friendly to Jesus, whose innocence is a matter of indifference to him. He hardly seeks to placate the Jews and avoid decision: "Rather, his aim is to humiliate 'the Jews' and to ridicule their national hopes by means of Jesus."[16] Indeed, he exacts a devastating price from them, bullying them into accepting the kingship of Caesar, and upon attaining this end he "hands over Jesus with alacrity." Thus, in this reading, Pilate is no "chameleon"[17] or fence-sitter, but consistently "callous and relentless, indifferent to Jesus and to truth, and contemptuous of the hope of Israel that Jesus both fulfills and transcends."[18] This interpretation is more in tune with what we know of the historical Pilate, who was eventually removed from office for his arrogant, bullying, offensive behavior.

Whatever the case may be, there is no denying that the trial of Jesus before Pilate takes center stage in John's account of Jesus' passion, thereby showcasing the intersection of religion and politics.[19] As Gail O'Day observes, "The portrait of the complicity of the Jewish leadership and the Roman procurator in John 18:28–19:16a may provide the most vibrant picture of any of the Gospels of the complex relationship of Jews and Romans in the decades leading up to the revolt of 70 CE."[20] It no doubt also provided instruction for John's community in its own dealings with Roman officials in the post-70 years. David Rensberger sees in the story a twofold thrust to this instruction that hardly advises retreat from political relationships: "On the one hand, confrontation with Rome is not avoided."[21] The first readers and hearers of this story had to decide whether Jesus was their king or whether Caesar was, and would have been reminded by it that "Rome has no authority of its own over those who are of God."[22] "On the other hand, it is exactly because the kingship of Jesus is not of this world that the confrontation between the two does not take place according to the standards of the world or according to its means." As Rensberger points out, Jesus, who is by no means submissive, is contrasted not only with Caesar but also with Barabbas, the "freedom fighter." Thus he models "an alternative to both zealotry and collaboration, by calling for adherence to the king who is not of this world, whose servants do not fight but remain in the world bearing witness to the truth before the rulers of both synagogue and Empire."[23]

The story continues to instruct disciples, for we too must negotiate the complex intersection of religion and politics. It prompts us to reconsider our own allegiances to God and to country, facing the question: to whom do we grant sovereignty over our lives? It calls into question our own political systems, reminding us that their power is limited to *this* world and to what God may grant (19:10–11). It continues to hold before us a devastating portrait of "religion that has lost its soul by compromise thinly veiled by empty ritual and false patriotism."[24] And it calls disciples of Jesus to live as a witnessing, alternative community in and for the world, embodying the standards of another world. Above all, it bears witness to the truly sovereign one who is alone worthy of our hearts' devotion and our lives' allegiance: God's own Son and true reflection, who has "conquered the world" (16:33) and grants us power to become children of God (1:12).

THE CRUCIFIXION AND BURIAL OF JESUS (19:16b–42)

John's emphasis on Jesus' sovereignty is further reflected in the account of the crucifixion and burial. There is no indication that the soldiers strip Jesus of his purple cloak (as in Mark 15:20; Matt. 27:31), so he approaches his death in royal garb, and to the end he remains fully in control of the events of his passion. On the way to Golgotha, he carries his own cross (19:17). The inscription that Pilate insists be affixed to it ("Jesus of Nazareth, the King of the Jews") is "written in Hebrew, in Latin, and in Greek"—a worldwide proclamation of his sovereignty (19:19–22). In his dying moments, he provides for his mother and his beloved disciple, entrusting them to each other's care (19:25–27), and thirsts to drink his cup of suffering to the full, thereby fulfilling the plan of God set forth in the Scriptures (19:28). He does not cry out to God in agony, wondering why he has been forsaken.[25] Instead, in control of his destiny to the end, he calmly announces "'It is finished.' Then he bowed his head and gave up his spirit" (19:30).

Jesus thus dies in a sovereign manner, and in death his body continues his salvific work, as blood and water flow from his pierced side (19:34), fulfilling his earlier prophecy ("From within him shall flow rivers of living water"; 7:38) and symbolizing the gift of the Spirit (7:39) that would be given upon his glorification.[26] Moreover, while the other Gospels also mark Jesus' death with miraculous signs (the Temple curtain is torn; tombs open and bodies of saints come forth; a Roman centurion is moved to expression of faith), only the Fourth Gospel localizes the sign in the body of Jesus himself.[27] Finally, Jesus is buried in "a new tomb in which no one had ever been laid" (19:41), wrapped in linen clothes with a staggering amount of spices ("a mixture of myrrh and aloes, weighing about a hundred pounds" (19:39)—in short, a burial fit for a king.[28]

In sum, John presents Jesus as sovereign in life and in death, from beginning to end, as he freely lays down his life in love for his friends. He has overcome the world (16:33), giving us eyes of faith to see "that suffering and evil have no real power over God's Son or over those whom he enables to become God's children."[29] Indeed, Raymond Brown maintains that "this is the narrative that has made Good Friday good. It is a narrative for all those who in the course of history have been persecuted by the powerful, but whose sense that God is with them has made them realize how little power any worldly authority really has. Those who believe in Jesus have eternal life, and like him they can say, 'No one takes it from me.'"[30]

There can be no doubt about the significance of the cross from John's perspective—for believers, and also for Jesus. It is, for us, a sign of the depths of God's love (3:16)—a love without limits—a love "to the end" (13:1).[31] No one has greater love than this (15:13). To John's way of thinking, the power of such love is irresistible, utterly compelling, drawing us to Christ like a magnet (12:32), and overcoming our alienation from God.[32] Moreover, it manifests a sovereignty like none we have ever seen, sustained not by coercion and violence but by suffering love.

The cross is no less significant for Jesus, for there his earthly sojourn comes to an end and his work is brought to completion, as the revelation of God's great love for us is fully visible for all to see. He is not destroyed by crucifixion, but by means of it "lifted up" from the earth (12:32–34), as he returns to God and to the glory that was his before creation.

QUESTIONS FOR DISCUSSION OR REFLECTION

Individually or as a group, read through John 18–19 and make a list of everything you find that conveys Jesus' sovereignty, his control of the events of his passion. Share your reaction to this emphasis.

What most captures your attention in John's story of Jesus' passion, and why?

What do you make of the striking presence of Roman soldiers in John's account of the arrest of Jesus?

In the account of the arrest of Jesus and Peter's denial, intriguing details appear, such as "lanterns and torches" (18:3) and "a charcoal fire" (18:18). And only in John is the slave who loses his ear identified by name as "Malchus" (18:10). What do you make of these details, or any others that catch your attention? Are any ironies implied?

Do a dramatic reading of the story of Jesus' trial before Pilate in 18:28–19:16. Assign roles to a narrator, to Jesus, and to Pilate, and have the rest of the group read collectively the lines of "the Jews," the chief priests, and the soldiers. Following the reading, debrief the roles: What struck you most about the role you were assigned? What struck you most about the roles of others? What questions does the story raise for you?

Do you think Pilate is presented as a weak character or a strong character? Which interpretation of him makes the most sense to you? (Note: some scholars believe 19:8 should be translated: "he became fearful instead" rather than "he was more afraid than ever.")[33]

Sometimes Jesus' affirmation in 18:36, "My kingdom is not from this world," has been used as a rationale for Christian disengagement from the world. What do you think about this?

How do you hear Pilate's question in 19:38: "What is truth?" What do you imagine his tone of voice to be? Do you think it is a serious philosophical query or a dismissive one? Does it give expression to genuine yearning or exasperation, in your view?

Who do you think is sitting on the judge's bench in 19:13: Pilate or Jesus?

What insights do you gain from the story of Jesus' trial before Pilate that can inform your own life of discipleship, your own negotiation of the complex intersection between religion and politics?

The differences among the four Gospels are due in large part to the fact that they were written to meet the pastoral needs of different Christian communities. Had you noticed these differences before? Do you find that they trouble or enrich your faith?

As a point of comparison, you may wish to examine the different words of Jesus from the cross (see Mark 15:34, paralleled in Matt. 27:46; Luke 23:34, 43, 46; John 19:26–27, 28, 30). Which of Jesus' seven words from the cross speaks most powerfully to you at this time in your life, and why?

A number of details in the crucifixion scene have no parallel in the other Gospels (e.g., the translation of the inscription over the cross into Hebrew, Latin, and Greek; the seamless tunic; the presence of Jesus' mother and the Beloved Disciple at the foot of the cross and Jesus' address to them; Jesus' words "I thirst" and "It is finished"; the flow of blood and water from Jesus' pierced side). What interests you most about these details, and why?

Mark's passion narrative presents a Jesus who is abandoned by his followers and has to face his hour alone, thus enduring the cross in a particularly agonizing way (Mark 14:27, 32–41, 50–52, 66–74; 15:25–32, 34). Matthew follows Mark closely, but introduces into the passion narrative the haunting issue of responsibility (Matt. 27:3–10, 19, 24–25). Luke emphasizes the compassionate, healing presence of Jesus throughout the passion narrative (Luke 22:51; 23:12, 28, 34, 42–43). John's Gospel emphasizes the sovereignty of Jesus. Raymond Brown points out that the presence in the canon of four diverse perspectives makes "it possible for people with very different spiritual needs to find meaning in the cross."[34] Consider his reflection on this point, and share your reaction to it:

> There are moments in the lives of most Christians when they need desperately to cry out with the Marcan/Matthean Jesus, "My God, my God, why have you forsaken me?" and to find, as Jesus did, that despite human appearances God is listening and can reverse tragedy. At other moments, meaning in suffering may be linked to being able to say with the Lucan Jesus, "Father, forgive them for they know not what they do," and being able to entrust oneself confidently to God's hands. There are still other moments where with Johannine faith we must see that suffering and evil have no real power over God's Son or over those whom he enables to become God's children. To choose one portrayal of the crucified Jesus in a manner that would exclude the other portrayals or to harmonize all the Gospel portrayals into one would deprive the cross of much of its meaning. It is important that some be able to see the head bowed in dejection, while others observe the arms outstretched in forgiveness, and still others perceive in the title on the cross the proclamation of a reigning king.[35]

What spiritual needs in your life or your congregation does John's story address?

When you think of the cross, do you think of it primarily as a sign of God's love? Why, or why not? What do you think of John's presentation of the cross in this way?

What new insights have emerged from your study of John's passion narrative or your group discussion of it?

12

Encounters with the Risen Lord

John 20

None of the Gospels provides an account of the resurrection of Jesus, but they do provide reports of the empty tomb and of the risen Lord's appearances to his disciples. The Gospel of John presents some of the most memorable of these stories, featuring a wide cast of characters with different faith reactions to the resurrection. That diversity is instructive, for as Fred Craddock notes, it is a reminder that "faith is not for all the same experience, neither is it generated for all with the same kind and degree of 'evidence.'"[1] The Gospel of John also maintains that faith is not limited to Jesus' original circle of disciples or to their experiences of the risen Christ.[2] It is available to us as well—indeed, to all persons in all times and places. Let us consider, then, how John's resurrection narratives can inform our own encounters with the risen Lord.

MARY MAGDALENE: WITNESS TO THE RESURRECTION (20:1–18)

Mary Magdalene first appears in John at the foot of the cross (19:25); but her primary role in this Gospel is that of witness to the resurrection. Before we turn to her story, however, it may be important to clear our heads of the interpretive litter that clouds her portrait. For centuries, artists, poets, preachers, and Hollywood producers alike have depicted her as a woman of considerable beauty, loose hair, loose morals, and exposed cleavage.

Have you ever thought of her in that way? If so, can you reach back in your memory and pinpoint how you made that connection? For me, it was a Broadway musical from the 1970s that did it: *Jesus Christ Superstar*. In this musical (and later movie), wildly popular during my teenage years, Mary Magdalene is depicted as singing this song: "I don't know how to love him—what to do, how to move him. He's a man—he's just a man—*and I've had so many men before in very many ways—he's just one more*" (italics mine). Andrew Lloyd Webber was responsible for warping my consciousness. Clearly, Webber was presenting the popular image of Mary Magdalene as a "repentant sinner, lifted from the depths of whoredom by her romantic love for Jesus."[3] Indeed, in the minds of many, she is first and foremost a prostitute, a repentant whore. But nowhere in the New Testament is she ever identified as such.

This misconception arises from fantasy and from the confusion or conflation of her portrait with that of other New Testament women. Sometimes she is mistakenly identified as the Samaritan woman (infamous for her five husbands; John 4) or as the woman caught in adultery (John 8). But the evangelist Luke is chiefly to blame for this confusion: in Luke 7:36–50 he tells the story of "a woman in the city, who was a sinner," who, in gratitude for forgiveness received, anoints Jesus' feet, wets them with her tears, and wipes them with her hair. The nature of that woman's sin is not specified, nor is she identified by name. One has to wonder why sexual sin is the only sin of which women are presumed to be capable and also why the anonymous sinful woman is presumed to be Mary Magdalene. The only reason for such an identification is that in the following chapter (Luke 8), Luke mentions a group of women who accompany Jesus and his disciples and "who provided for them out of their resources," one of whom is "Mary, called Magdalene, from whom seven demons had gone out" (8:1–3). However, she is not identified as the anonymous woman in Luke 7, and nowhere in the New Testament is demon possession equated with sexual sin. In short, the presumption that Mary Magdalene was a prostitute has no biblical foundation.

When we consider what the Gospels actually have to say about her, a rather different portrait emerges: she was one of Christ's female followers (Luke 8:1–3); she was present at his crucifixion (Mark 15:40–41, 47; Matt. 27:55–56, 61; Luke 23:49–56; John 19:25); she was a witness of his resurrection (Mark 16:1–8; Matt. 28:1–10; Luke 24:1–11; John 20:1–18); and, according to both John and Matthew, she was the first to be charged with the supreme ministry of proclaiming the Christian message (Matt. 28:1–10; John 20:1–18).[4] Therefore, setting interpretive litter aside, let us attend closely to John's distinctive story of Mary Magdalene's encounter with the risen Lord.

In the Gospel of John, Mary Magdalene is the very picture of devotion. She comes alone to Jesus' tomb on Easter morning, "while it was still dark," and finds the stone removed (20:1). "So she ran and went to Simon Peter and the other disciple, the one whom Jesus loved, and said to them, 'They have taken the Lord out of the tomb, and we do not know where they have laid him'" (20:2). She assumes the body has been stolen, perhaps by Roman soldiers, Jewish opponents, or grave robbers. Her report prompts a race back to the tomb, where Jesus' grave clothes are discovered and described in some detail (20:5–7). The careful description of them brings to mind the grave clothes of Lazarus, which still bound him tightly as he emerged from his tomb (11:44). Jesus' grave clothes, however, have been left behind—he will never need them again! We are told by John that the beloved disciple "saw and believed" (20:8), but that neither he nor Simon Peter yet understood the Scripture's witness to Jesus' resurrection from the dead (20:9).

So what, exactly, did the beloved disciple "believe" (20:8) since he is also described, curiously, as "not understanding" the Scripture's witness to resurrection (20:9)? Sandra Schneiders sheds light on this enigma by noting that the Gospel of John distinguishes between Jesus' glorification (which takes place on the cross when Jesus goes to the Father) and his resurrection (by which the glorified Jesus returns to his own).[5] As she explains, the beloved disciple comes to belief in the former, Jesus' glorification and return to God, when he sees the "face veil" that Jesus left behind in the tomb (20:7–8). The veil is a "sign" for him of Jesus' glorification because Moses also put aside the veil covering his face when he ascended to meet God in glory (Exod. 34:33–35).[6] But the beloved disciple has not yet come to belief in the latter, Jesus' resurrection or return to his own. That recognition awaits Jesus' appearance to him in the second half of this chapter (John 20:19–23).

Thus both the beloved disciple and Peter return to their homes (20:10), where they will soon huddle behind locked doors in fear (20:19). "But Mary stood weeping outside the tomb" (20:11)—a lone woman, depicted as wandering in a darkened garden, questioning strangers, intent upon finding the dead body of her Lord. As her story resumes and unfolds, it is characterized by three central movements: that of "weeping," "turning," and "announcing."[7]

"Weeping" governs the first movement of the story (vv. 11–15; see

vv. 11, 13, 15). Mary Magdalene is overcome with sorrow, blinded by grief, so much so that she is apparently unperturbed by the appearance in the tomb of two angels. Angelic appearances in the New Testament are usually greeted with considerable fear and astonishment (cf. Mark 16:1–8). But Mary is so intent on her mission and so overcome with sorrow that she is unfazed even as they address her, challenging the basis of her sorrow: "They said to her, 'Woman, why are you weeping?' She said to them, 'They have taken away my Lord, and I do not know where they have laid him'" (v. 13).

The risen Lord himself then appears, and asks the same question: "Woman, why are you weeping?" and also asks, "Whom are you looking for?" (v. 15). The first words of the risen Lord echo the first words he uttered at the beginning of the Gospel of John ("What are you looking for?"; 1:38). What or whom are *we* looking for? This question of invitation frames this Gospel and is asked of every one of us who enters it. It is a question that asks us to discern and articulate our deepest longings, longings that, to John's way of thinking, are addressed ultimately and fully only by encounter with God in Christ. Mary Magdalene, however, remains blinded by grief, even as the risen Lord himself addresses her. Indeed, "She did not know that it was Jesus" (v. 14); and "Supposing him to be the gardener, she said to him, 'Sir, if you have carried him away, tell me where you have laid him, and I will take him away'" (v. 15). To her way of thinking, Jesus' dead body is all that remains of his presence to her and to the world, and she persists in her effort to locate it, so that she may "take him away."

"Turning," however, constitutes the second movement of the text and signals a change in her perspective, indeed a conversion.[8] It is accomplished by a single word: "Jesus said to her, 'Mary!' She turned and said to him in Hebrew, 'Rabbouni!' (which means Teacher)" (v. 16). He calls her by name, for he is the Good Shepherd "who calls his own sheep by name and leads them out" (10:3). The moment illustrates his claim: "I am the good shepherd. I know my own and my own know me" (10:14). Hearing the risen Lord call her name, Mary finds her sorrow dispelled, her vision transformed, and her life graced with new possibilities by the reality of the resurrection.

But she still has an important resurrection lesson to learn about the nature of Jesus' continued presence in the lives of believers. He will no longer be physically present to them. Thus when she moves to embrace him, he says to her: "Do not hold on to me, because I have not yet ascended to the Father" (v. 17). The words are not as harsh as they may at first sound. Jesus does not prohibit Mary from "touching" him (see 20:27), but from "holding on" or "clinging" to him. As commentator Gail O'Day explains, the Greek verb for "hold" (*haptō*) has connotations of physical holding, but also communicates a broader range of meaning: "To hold onto something is to control, to own, to define, to manipulate, to manage, to co-opt for one's own ends."[9] In truth, Jesus is teaching Mary the first post-resurrection lesson: "Jesus cannot and will not be held and controlled."[10] This point is an important one for us, too, to grasp: "Jesus cannot be contained or identified through our labels and categories."[11] Indeed, "we come to know who Jesus is only when we allow Jesus to be Jesus and stop holding him to who we want him to be."[12] Archbishop of Canterbury Rowan Williams provides further reflection on Jesus' injunction along similar lines:

> There is a clinging to Jesus that shows itself in the longing to be utterly sure of our rightness. We want him where we can see him and manage him, so that we know exactly where to turn to be told that everything is all right and that he is on our side. We do it in religious conflicts, we do it in moral debates, and we do it in politics. We want to stand still and be reassured, rather than moving faithfully with Jesus along a path into new life whose turnings we don't know in advance. . . . Perhaps when Jesus tells us not to cling to him, one of the many things he says is, "Do not use me, do not use any vision of what is true or good, to keep yourself from recognizing the real and potential evil within you. Don't cling; follow. Take the next step, putting your feet in the gap I have cleared, conscious of how you may make mistakes, but trusting that I can restore you and lead you further, that I can deal with the residues of evil in your heart and in every heart."[13]

Moreover, Mary Magdalene and believers are given to understand that after Jesus' ascension to the Father, his continued presence in the world will be by means of the Spirit (John 14–16; see especially 16:20–24).

In the final movement of this text, Jesus redirects Mary's attention to the community of believers where his spiritual presence abides.[14] "Weeping" and "turning" give way to "announcing," to mission: "Do not hold on to me. . . . But go to my brothers and sisters and say to them, 'I am ascending to my Father and your Father, to my God and your God'" (v. 17). These words of commission capture, in a nutshell, John's understanding of the good news of Easter: as a result of Jesus' life, death, resurrection, and ascension, a new relationship with God is available. "My Father" is now "your Father"; "my God" is now "your God";

and Jesus' Spirit now unites believers to him and to one another as "brothers and sisters." The Word became flesh in this world in order that all who receive him and believe in his name might be given power "to become children of God" (1:12). That work is accomplished through his life, death, and resurrection, and the power of his Spirit. This gospel is entrusted to Mary, and in obedience to her commission, "Mary Magdalene went and announced to the disciples, 'I have seen the Lord'; and she told them that he had said these things to her" (v. 18). Interestingly, the words "I have seen the Lord" are the very words Paul uses in basing his claim to apostleship on a vision of the risen Lord (1 Cor. 9:1). Mary clearly "fits Paul's criterion for apostleship" and "was sent with a message that provided the foundation for the community."[15]

But sadly, the appearance of the risen Lord to Mary Magdalene has often been trivialized as of lesser importance than his appearance to the male disciples—indeed, "as a minor, private, personal, or unofficial encounter between Jesus and his (hysterical?) female follower, in which he kindly consoles her before making his official and public Easter appearances to male witnesses and commissioning them to carry on his mission in the world."[16] On the contrary, Mary Magdalene is, from John's perspective, the official Easter witness in and to John's community[17]—and to us. She is, indeed, "the personification of all that it means to be a disciple."[18] May John's portrait of her courage, devotion, and faith inspire us to live also as joyful witnesses to the resurrection.

THE DISCIPLES: BEHIND LOCKED DOORS (20:19–23)

The first half of John's resurrection narrative portrays the events of Easter morning: the finding of the empty tomb, and the first appearance of the risen Lord to Mary Magdalene (20:1–18). It is to a woman that Jesus first appears, instructing her to go and tell his other disciples of his ascension to the Father. The second half of John's resurrection narrative turns to Jesus' subsequent appearance to those other disciples on Easter evening. It is worth noting that the appearance to Mary Magdalene and the appearance to the other disciples are back-to-back, and that while a lone woman has been roaming in a darkened cemetery, questioning strangers, searching for the missing body of her Lord, the disciples are huddled behind "locked" doors "for fear of the Jews" (20:19). With these not so subtle details in verse 19, John paints a portrait of the disciples as engulfed in fear.

"Fear of the Jews" may seem odd, as the disciples themselves are Jews. The reference no doubt reflects the fear experienced by the community to which John's Gospel was first addressed—fear, in particular, of the Jewish religious authorities in their vicinity, and of the larger unbelieving world they came to represent for the Fourth Evangelist. John's early Christian community probably suffered expulsion from the synagogue for their confession of faith (9:22, 34; 12:42; 16:2). Thus a difficult historical process of separation and self-differentiation accounts for the disciples' fear—a process that is now well behind us. The church no longer gathers behind locked doors "for fear of the Jews"; though in our day, Jews might well find reason to lock synagogue doors for fear of Christians. Fear, however, is a reality with which disciples throughout the ages struggle as they face the unbelieving world around them in whatever forms it takes, and John's portrait of cowering disciples prompts us to name the things that frighten and demoralize us in our own particular contexts.

Fear, it seems, can paralyze us even on an Easter evening when news of resurrection is abroad. The disciples, after all, have heard Mary Magdalene's testimony but respond by going into protective seclusion, shutting out all threats of the world's hostility. To their credit, they are still together, united in their shared fear and paralyzed state.[19] But they do not yet realize that a new life awaits them beyond closed doors. The one who earlier had described himself saying, "I am the door" (10:7), must summon them again to the abundant fullness of life available to them. Indeed, their life of continuing discipleship, as John portrays it, will depend completely on Christ's faithfulness and initiative.

Thus "Jesus came and stood among them" (20:19). The risen Christ enters rooms locked by fear, meeting disciples in the midst of their condition, with three results. The first is peace, for twice the risen Christ addresses them saying, "Peace be with you" (20:19, 21). These words represent much more than a greeting or a wish, but rather a statement of fact and fulfillment of a promise made during their last meal together: "Peace I leave with you; my peace I give to you. I do not give to you as the world gives. Do not let your hearts be troubled, and do not let them be afraid" (14:27). Now he fulfills that promise, transforming the situation of his followers with a gift of peace.

But to what, exactly, does this gift refer? It can hardly connote inner calm or exemption from suffering and conflict, for the disciples have been forewarned that they are likely to encounter the world's hatred and persecution (15:18–16:4)—that they can expect the same reception in the world that was accorded their master. But the world will not have the last word, for as Jesus spoke of his final hour at their final meal together he also promised: "I have said this to you, so that in me you may have peace. In the world you face persecution. But take courage; I have conquered the world!" (16:33). The peace that Jesus gives to his disciples is thus the fruit of the decisive victory over the unbelieving world and the powers of evil that his cross represents. Indeed, it is as the disciples behold the wounds of the cross in his hands and side—wounds made by Roman nails and a Roman spear—that their fear is transformed into joy and gladness. In view of these wounds, they can rest assured that whatever the world inflicts upon them, it will not ultimately undo them. The peace that Jesus gives is also clearly the gift of his enduring presence with his disciples and the church. For in the Holy Spirit, which he will also soon give, they are assured that God in Christ will always be with them in all their involvement in the world. Thus the power of Christ's life and death, his victory over all that threatens them, and the power of his enduring and sustaining presence drive away the disciples' fear and bring peace.

The gift of Christ's peace, however, is not for disciples alone, for they are to bear it into the life of the world. Indeed, the second immediate result of the risen Lord's appearance to them is mission. Their fear now addressed and peace conferred, the disciples are promptly commissioned, dispatched, pushed right out the door—back into the world—as in one powerful sentence the risen Christ joins the mission of the church to his own mission: "As the Father has sent me, so I send you" (20:21; see also 17:18). Remarkably, the disciples' mission is to continue the Son's own mission, through which God, out of love, seeks to rescue the world from its plight, to salvage a distorted creation.[20] They are to be for the world as he was.

It is a uniquely Johannine contribution to the church's understanding of its mission, and an utterly astonishing one. Jesus was sent as the Lamb of God, to take away the sin of the world (1:29), and now the disciples are to continue that work. And how does that take place? It is important to recall that "sin," in John, refers not to moral transgressions but to unbelief (e.g., 16:8–9), blindness to the revelation of God in Christ (John 9); and throughout the Fourth Gospel, Jesus so mirrors God that people who encounter him are forced to make a decision. What will be their response to the revelation of God in Christ: belief or unbelief? That response will determine how they themselves will be judged (3:16–19). In like manner, disciples are to so mirror Jesus that those who encounter them are forced to make a decision in their lives, forced to self-judgment. They will re-present Christ, and this will call forth a response, a decision that will determine whether sins are forgiven or retained (20:23).[21]

Mutual love among Christians and their unity with one another are clearly essential to this missionary task of mirroring Jesus. As Jesus said during his Farewell Discourse, "By this everyone will know that you are my disciples, if you have love for one another" (13:35). And in his final prayer for his disciples, he beseeched the Father that they would "become completely one, so that the world may know that you have sent me and have loved them even as you have loved me" (17:23). As Mortimer Arias observes, it is a decidedly "incarnational" understanding of mission,[22] in which the life of love becomes "the trademark and credential of the missionary community."[23] It is, moreover, a stunning, even startling view of the church as the locus of the continuing manifestation of God in Christ.[24]

This re-presenting of Jesus requires that he be present to his disciples during this mission, and thus they are given the gift of the Holy Spirit. This is the third result of their encounter with the risen Lord, for after commissioning them, "he breathed on them and said to them, 'Receive the Holy Spirit'" (20:22). There we have it: the Johannine Pentecost, brief as it is. It lacks the flair of Luke's dramatic account in Acts 2, but earlier in John Jesus provided considerable commentary on what receiving the Holy Spirit would mean in his farewell conversations, when he spoke to the disciples about the coming of the Paraclete (14:16–17, 25–26; 15:26–27; 16:7–15). In those passages, the Spirit/Paraclete clearly emerges as a personal presence—"the ongoing presence of Jesus while he is absent from the earth and with the Father in heaven."[25] The Spirit is present, for example, as a comforter in times of trouble or sorrow; as a teacher, bringing to our remembrance all that Jesus said and did, and revealing the mind of Christ in new situations; and as an advocate, standing beside believers when they are called upon to defend their faith or to speak truth to those who hold power, empowering unwavering witness.

In "breathing" upon the disciples, Jesus quite literally "inspires" the church for its mission. The verb "to breathe" (*emphysaō* in Greek) appears only here in the New Testament, and evokes God's breath in the creation scene in Genesis 2:7. Indeed, the same verb appears in Genesis 2:7 in the Septuagint, the Greek translation of the Old Testament. Thus we are given to understand that just as in the first creation God breathed a living spirit into the human being, so now in the moment of new creation Jesus breathes his Holy Spirit into the disciples. The same breath that brought Adam to his feet now also sends the disciples out the door, for the gift of the Holy Spirit is not an experience disciples keep for themselves; it is equipment for mission.[26]

In sum, through the initiative and faithfulness of the risen Christ, the disciples find themselves equipped with his peace, with his Spirit, with his word of commission, and freed from fear of all that threatens them. They are freed to unlock the doors and bear witness in the world—to be for the world as he was.

THOMAS: MISSING OUT ON THE RESURRECTION (20:24–31)

Not all of Jesus' disciples were present for the risen Lord's appearance on Easter eve, however. At least Thomas was absent, and so the disciples told him, "We have seen the Lord" (20:25). But Thomas needed convincing, stating rather emphatically: "Unless I see the mark of the nails in his hands, and put my finger in the mark of the nails and my hand in his side, I will not believe" (20:25). Thus, a week later, when the disciples were gathered once again, the risen Lord came and stood among them a second time, graciously offering exactly what Thomas claimed he needed to believe: "Put your finger here and see my hands. Reach out your hand and put it in my side" (20:27).

Thomas has long been unjustly maligned as a "doubter," when in fact his situation is no different than that of his fellow disciples. They apparently did not believe upon hearing Mary Magdalene's testimony to the resurrection; they too had to see the risen Lord for themselves to believe. Thomas's insistence that he share their experience is an understandable one. Moreover, the Greek verb for "doubt" (*distazō*) does not actually appear in the text (in the New Testament, only Matthew employs this verb, in Matt. 14:31 and 28:17). A literal translation of Jesus' exhortation to Thomas in John 20:27 would read: "Do not be unbelieving (*apistos*) but believing (*pistos*)."

Moreover, Thomas speaks for all of us who missed out on the first resurrection appearances.[27] In a sense, he takes words we might like to say right out of our mouths.[28] We can also be grateful to Thomas for raising a crucial question for faith. How can we be sure that the one who appeared in the disciples' midst was not a phantom, an apparition, rather than the crucified man Jesus? Thomas insists that there must be continuity between the dead one and the living one if he is to believe, and in insisting on this continuity, he puts his finger on a critical matter (no pun intended). As Wellford Hobbie observes, "The ultimate question is not whether there is someone or something out there in limitless space whom we call God, but whether there is someone who knows something of the dust of the earth, something of the blood-stained face human existence wears, and can feel for it."[29] In like manner, William Temple wrote: "The wounds of Christ are his credentials to the suffering race of humanity."[30] Again taking the initiative, the risen Christ appears once more in the midst of his disciples, and invites Thomas to experience what he claimed he needed. He shows his wounds a second time, so that both Thomas and we may know that the one who lives is also the one who was slain and that "he bears forever on his body the marks of wounded humanity."[31] We do not know whether Thomas touched the wounds, but we do know that in full recognition of them, he utters the Gospel's climactic confession: "My Lord and my God!" (20:28).

No more profound confession is uttered in any Gospel. Indeed, Thomas is the first person to look at Jesus and address him directly as "God."[32] Resurrection is a sign to him, and to us all, of Jesus' return to God and to the glory that was his before creation. Thus in this dead one raised we experience the ultimate divine reality—our Lord and our God. It is the point the evangelist John has been working around to from the beginning, when he introduced the Word who "was with God" and "was God" (1:1) and who "became flesh and lived among us" (1:14). To make this confession is to acknowledge the full revelation of God in Jesus Christ, and to pledge one's loyalty to him above any other "lords" or "Caesars." It is not an idle pledge, for Thomas makes it "deep in Caesar's territory,"[33] acknowledging that Jesus alone is worthy of his heart's full devotion and his life's ultimate allegiance.

Thomas speaks on behalf of the whole Christian community, even on behalf of those of us in subsequent generations who have not seen the wounds and yet believe. Because just as Jesus transformed Thomas's doubt and disbelief into faith, so he continues to care for us, to offer himself to us, and to evoke faith in us through the church's preaching, teaching, and witness. His word of peace, the breath of his Spirit, and his word of commission move and empower us too, and we are assured that our faith is no less real than that of the first disciples—that we are by no means second-class Christians. Indeed, the risen Jesus' final words in this scene are for us: "Blessed are those who have not seen and yet have come to believe" (20:29).

The Fourth Gospel itself is a continuing means by which we encounter the grace of God in Jesus Christ. Indeed, as it nears its close, the evangelist identifies this as his purpose in writing: "Now Jesus did many other signs in the presence of his disciples, which are not written in this book. But these are written so that you may come to believe that Jesus is the Messiah, the Son of God, and that through believing you may have life in his name" (20:30–31). An interesting difference in wording appears in the ancient manuscripts at this point that involves the presence or absence of a single Greek letter. Thus we are not sure whether these things are written that we may "come to believe" (*pisteusēte*) or that we may "go on believing" (*pisteuēte*); that is, whether the evangelist's purpose in writing is to evangelize and convert nonbelievers or rather to nurture and edify the faith of believers. Throughout the ages, however, the Fourth Gospel has admirably served both ends. Indeed, it has proved to have authority in believers' lives because it both authors a new identity for them as God's own children and sustains them in it. Through its continuing witness to Jesus Christ may we too come to know and live more fully into the rich quality of life that emerges from that intimate relationship.

QUESTIONS FOR DISCUSSION OR REFLECTION

Before beginning your study of John 20, share briefly: What impressions of Mary Magdalene do you bring with you to your study of John 20? When you think of her, what images come to mind, and why? In popular imagination, she has been depicted throughout the centuries as a repentant whore. Have you ever thought of her in this way?

Do a dramatic reading of 20:1–18. Assign roles to a narrator, to Jesus, to Mary Magdalene, and to the two angels. Following the reading, share briefly: What most captures your attention as you hear the story? What questions does the story raise for you?

What do you make of the race to the tomb in 20:3–8, particularly the fact that the beloved disciple is the first to arrive at the tomb, but Peter the first to enter it (20:3–8)? To your way of thinking, what does this convey?

Noting the distinction that John makes between Jesus' glorification and resurrection, John Wronski poses an interesting question: "Do you think that some contemporary Christians, like the disciples, find it easy to affirm that Jesus is personally glorified but not to believe that he is truly risen, that is, that he has returned to his disciples, that he is alive with us today?"[34]

How would you answer Jesus' question, "Whom [or What] are you looking for?" (1:38; 20:15).

In your own experience of grief, what angels or gardeners—powerful or ordinary witnesses—opened your eyes to the possibility of new life?

John is the only Gospel that explicitly identifies the site of Jesus' burial as a "garden" (19:41), and Mary mistakes Jesus for a "gardener" (20:15). Some discern connections with another garden in Genesis 1. Do you? If so, what do you think this conveys about Jesus' resurrection? Is the evangelist suggesting, perhaps, that Jesus represents the beginning of a new creation?

What do you make of Jesus' much-discussed injunction: "Do not hold on to me" (20:17)? Banalities abound: some propose "romantic" interpretations of this admonition; others have even suggested that Jesus did not wish to be touched because his wounds were still sore. How would you interpret this admonition?

One way to interpret Jesus' injunction in 20:17 is in terms of the broader connotations of "holding" or "clinging." What are some of the ways in which we might attempt to "hold on" to Jesus—to "define" and "control" him?

What does the Gospel of John contribute to your understanding of Mary Magdalene? How can John's portrait of her inform your own discipleship?

What does John's portrait of Mary Magdalene suggest about the role of women in the ancient and contemporary church, in your view? Why do you think she has been depicted throughout the centuries as a repentant whore? Some scholars believe this legendary transformation of her "reflects a Christian reaction against female power and the authority of this major witness to the crucial data of Christianity, especially the resurrection."[35] What do you think about this?

The Gospel of John is remarkable for its intentional presentation of women as models of faith. Of all the women's portraits presented in John (John 2, 4, 8, 11, 12, 20), which has made the deepest impression on you, and why?

Do a dramatic reading of 20:19–31. Assign roles to a narrator, to Jesus, and to Thomas. Have the rest of the group read collectively the lines of the disciples. Following the reading, share briefly: What most captures your attention as you hear the story? What questions does it raise for you?

Like the first disciples, we too may find ourselves afraid, wanting to lock the doors and shut the world out, though realities that evoke our fear may differ. With what fears do you or your community of faith struggle as you face the unbelieving world around you? Try to name the things that frighten and demoralize you in your own particular context.

What do you learn from John 20 about the gift of Christ's peace? When have you experienced the gift of which he speaks? How does it bear on the realities you identified above?

What strikes you most about John's brief and condensed "Great Commission" in 20:21? What do you learn from it about the church's mission? If, as Mortimer Arias suggests, it is a decidedly "incarnational" paradigm of mission, what implications does this have for your life and ministry and that of your faith community?

What strikes you most about John's Pentecost scene in 20:22?

What impressions of Thomas do you bring to your reading of this story? What new insights about him emerge from your study or discussion? Would you describe him as "doubting"? Why, or why not?

Is Thomas's confession, "My Lord and my God!" (20:28), one that you share? What does this confession mean to you?

John 20 presents a wide cast of characters with different faith reactions to the resurrection. What evidence, in particular, seems to generate faith for each of them? What evidence, in particular, generated your own faith in Jesus' resurrection?

Of all the characters in John 20, with whom do you most identify, and why?

What questions would you like to ask Jesus, Mary Magdalene, the disciples, or Thomas?

What does the evangelist's statement of purpose in 20:30–31 suggest to you about the "authority" of Scripture and your engagement with it?

13

Unfinished Business

John 21

John 21 is an enigma of sorts. For one thing, it disrupts the sense of closure provided by the preceding chapter, where resurrection appearances, commissioning, a climactic confession ("My Lord and my God!"), and an authorial statement of purpose (20:30–31) appear to bring the Gospel to a fitting conclusion. Moreover, the scenario it narrates follows oddly on the heels of those dramatic, culminating events, for the disciples give no evidence of having experienced them. Though commissioned and empowered by the risen Lord in chapter 20, chapter 21 finds the disciples returning, aimlessly it seems, to Galilee to go fishing, and they do not recognize Jesus when he reappears. One can understand why most scholars believe John 21 to be an epilogue appended to the Gospel by a later editorial hand.

However, the Fourth Gospel has never circulated without it. Moreover, anticlimactic though it may be, it ties up a number of loose ends. Readers may be left wondering, for example, how Jesus dealt with the matter of Peter's denials. What does one say to a friend who betrayed you on the worst day of both your lives? And what became of Jesus' "beloved disciple"? Surely the Gospel would not end without appropriate recognition of the one closest to him. And what exactly does it mean to be "sent" by the risen Lord? What specific tasks are entailed in the discharge of this calling? John 21 addresses such unfinished business. Indeed, there is a sense in which the Fourth Gospel has two endings. The first, in John 20, brings the story of Jesus' life, death, and resurrec-

tion to a close. The second, in John 21, confirms that the story continues to this day in the ongoing ministry of the community of disciples.

FISHING INSTRUCTIONS (21:1–14)

What are disciples to do after Easter as the *alleluias* wane? Simon Peter's
response, "I am going fishing," would appear to illustrate the all-too-
familiar state of "post-Easter decline."[1] To be fair, we are not told of his
motivation or that of his fellow disciples who insist on joining him in
this venture. Are they in denial? In a state of disorientation? The Fourth
Gospel nowhere mentions that the disciples were fishermen by profession but may be familiar with that tradition, and after the life-shatter-
ing events of an intense week in Jerusalem one could understand an
inclination to gravitate back toward Galilee and mundane reality—
toward something, anything, still known for sure. And to be realistic,
disciples do have to eat. Still, fishing is not the noble endeavor we might
have anticipated for them as the upshot of resurrection and commission,
and it does not appear to be undertaken with any expectation of engagement with or on behalf of a risen Lord. Indeed, they seem to have
returned to their earlier circumstances, as if Jesus had never been.[2]

So the disciples go fishing—night fishing, a common practice—
though one wonders whether anything good can happen in John at
night (see John 3:2, 19–21; 11:10; 13:21–30; 18:15–27).[3] Apparently
not, for the fishing trip is a disaster: "they caught nothing" (21:3). Just
after daybreak, Jesus appears on the beach, unrecognized by the disciples. First, he elicits from them an acknowledgment of their failure.
Then he provides fishing instructions, urging them to cast the net to the
right side of the boat, with the result that "now they were not able to
haul it in because there were so many fish" (v. 6). It is not the first time
the disciples have found themselves face-to-face with a sign of such
abundance. Indeed, Jesus inaugurated his public ministry at a wedding
in Cana by producing an extravagant amount of wine. This concluding
sign of abundance leads immediately to the beloved disciple's recognition of the stranger standing on the beach: "It is the Lord!" (v. 7).

"When Simon Peter heard that it was the Lord, he put on some clothes,
for he was naked, and jumped into the sea" (v. 7). It seems an odd thing
to do—to add layers of clothing before swimming—and thus has given
rise to considerable speculation. Perhaps Peter clothes himself out of
respect for the risen Lord, in order to greet him properly. Or perhaps it

signifies that the shame of his denials weighs upon him, in contrast to Adam and Eve before the fall, who were "naked and unashamed" (Gen. 2:25).[4] Could it even be a sign that Peter is resisting the intimacy of nakedness before his Lord, just as he resisted foot washing, despite the Lord's own disrobing before his disciples in that earlier scene (13:4)?[5] Some point out that the adjective conveying that Peter was "naked" (*gymnos* in Greek) can also mean "lightly clad." Even so, other connections with the foot washing have been discerned, for only in these two places does the Greek verb for (literally) "girding" or "tucking" appear to describe the adjustment of clothing. Thus, just as Jesus is described as "girding" or "tying" a towel around himself, so Peter is described as "girding" or "tucking" his clothing. Perhaps it is a sign that he is ready to serve Jesus, as Jesus served him.[6] Or maybe we are straining a point and he "tucks" up his clothing simply in order to facilitate ease of movement in the water. Whatever the case may be, Peter's impetuous behavior certainly conveys his eagerness to reach the Lord. He quite literally goes overboard. In so doing, he also effects the total immersion he desired earlier: "Lord, not my feet only but also my hands and my head!" (13:9). The other disciples are left to drag the net full of fish to shore.

When they arrive ashore, they find that fish are already grilling upon a charcoal fire. Jesus instructs them to bring some of the fish they had caught, and though the disciples had not been able to drag the net into the boat, Simon Peter now single-handedly hauls the net ashore, "full of large fish, a hundred fifty-three of them; and though there were so many, the net was not torn" (v. 11). The precise number of fish is a conundrum of long standing and teases the minds of interpreters to this day. Surely it must bear some significance, for the Gospels are not given to extraneous picturesque details, though to date there is no consensus on what that significance might be. In the fourth century, Jerome, the most learned biblical scholar in the Latin church, contended that Greek zoologists had classified 153 species of fish, and that the number thus anticipates the inclusion of all types of people in the church's mission. In the fifth century, Saint Augustine, one of the greatest minds and influences in Christian history, took a mathematical approach, noting that the sum of all the numbers from 1 to 17 equals 153. It is not altogether clear why this is important, but since 17 is the sum of 10 plus 7, Augustine took the numbers as signifying the Ten Commandments and seven gifts of the Spirit, concluding that the total number of fish conveys the fulfillment of the law through the Spirit. However, he also conceded that the number 153 is "a great mystery."[7] Other mathematical speculations have centered on the significance of the numbers 100 + 50 + 3 (according to Cyril of Alexandria, for example, 100 represents the fullness of the Gentiles, 50 the remnant of Israel, and 3 the Holy Trinity).[8] More recently, the number has been taken as a sign of fulfillment, for in the prophet Ezekiel's vision of the age of salvation, people will be able to catch fish in the Dead Sea "from En-gedi to En-eglaim" (Ezek. 47:10), and the numerical value of the letters in the names of these two towns totals 17 and 153, respectively.[9] Of course it is possible that 153 represents eyewitness testimony (assuming that someone took the time to count all 153 fish). Or maybe the point is a much simpler one: that miraculously, the net was not torn, even though there were a whole lot of fish.

If there is any general agreement to be had among interpreters, it is that the fishing story as a whole conveys significant affirmations about the church's mission. The collective impact of many of the text's details point in this direction. Most obviously, in early Christian tradition, the catching of fish came to symbolize the church's mission of "catching people" (e.g., Luke 5:10; Mark 1:17). Moreover, the verb used to describe the hauling in of the net (*helkō*, vv. 6, 11) is used elsewhere in the Gospel to describe the drawing of people to Jesus (6:44; 12:32). The earlier references spoke of this drawing as the work of the Father and of Jesus himself, and John 21 intimates that after the resurrection disciples now join in that work.

That mission is represented as a communal undertaking (vv. 2–3), but one that remains utterly dependent on Jesus' initiative and empowering presence. Indeed, Teresa Okure finds the central theme of John 21 best summed up by Jesus' assertion in 15:5c: "apart from me you can do nothing."[10] Thus, when disciples undertake their project in the absence of Jesus ("at night") and without reference to him ("I am going fishing"), they catch "nothing" (v. 3) and must acknowledge the futility of their toil (v. 5).[11] But mission pursued under Jesus' guidance in obedience to his command is fruitful, abundantly so. Likewise, on their own strength, disciples cannot haul the net into the boat (v. 6), but at Jesus' command Peter can accomplish this task single-handedly (v. 11).

The scope, diversity, and success of the church's mission in the world are also in view, anticipated by the abundant catch of fish. The catch is so large it might well have broken the net, but it does not. Indeed, it is pointedly noted that there is no "schism" in the net (*schizō* in Greek, v. 11). In spite of the variety and number of persons drawn into the community of disciples, its basic unity is not destroyed. This too is a miracle, a gift of God to the church that resides in Jesus Christ, who continues to pray for the unity of his followers (17:20–26). Indeed, the ongoing struggle of the church to live into the fullness of that gift is integral to the church's continued ministry in mission in the world, and the reason why Jesus prayed that believers might "all be one. As you, Father, are in me and I am in you, may they also be in us, so that the world may believe that you have sent me" (17:21).

Significantly, the Fourth Gospel does not include a departure scene in which Jesus takes leave of his disciples (as in the Gospel of Luke, for example, where "he withdrew from them and was carried up into heaven"; Luke 24:51). Instead, as this Gospel comes to a close, Jesus is still among his disciples in the midst of their toil, forever surprising them with his presence.[12] Moreover, he continues to nourish and sustain them from his limitless supply of provisions, giving life in abundance. As he promised earlier, "Whoever comes to me will never be hungry" (6:35). Thus, just as he fed five thousand by the sea earlier in his ministry (John 6), he now hosts a breakfast, continuing to provide for his people after the resurrection. That this final meal is a morning breakfast rather than an evening supper suggests that there is a day ahead, work to do, a mission to accomplish, for which the meal will strengthen them.[13] "Jesus came and took the bread and gave it to them, and did the same with the fish" (v. 13), evoking the central table in the worship of the church, where believers continue to experience his provision and presence. All in all, it is a fitting inauguration of the church's mission, for as Gail O'Day observes, "Just as Jesus' ministry was inaugurated with a miracle of unprecedented abundance (2:1–11), so, too, is the church's ministry. John 21:1–14 . . . demonstrates for the community that its life is grounded in an experience of God's fullness and unprecedented, unexpected gift."[14]

PORTRAITS IN MINISTRY (21:15–25)

In the second half of John 21, attention turns from the collective mission engaged by the community as a whole to the diverging roles that two prominent disciples are to play within it. Moreover, the imagery and vocabulary of vocation shifts from that of fishing to shepherding, and thus from mission (bringing people into the community) to pastoral ministry (ongoing care and nurture of those within it). Those who shepherd, however, do not take up their vocation apart from the reality of forgiveness, and Peter must face his apostasy in order to move beyond it and take up his particular calling.

Peter must have known that a reckoning was coming, seated as he was before another charcoal fire. He had warmed himself before just such a fire on the night of his denials, desertion, and failure. After breakfast, Jesus placed before Peter a painful question, repeated three times—as many times as Peter had denied him: "Simon son of John, do you love me more than these?" (v. 15). It is one of the few times that Jesus uses Peter's whole name. (When our parents use our entire names, we know a serious matter is at hand.) It is perhaps also worth noting what Jesus does *not* say to Peter. He does not speak directly of Peter's spectacular failure or ask for an apology.[15] The question, instead, is "do you love me more than these?"

More than what? More than the boat and nets that belong to the life of a fisherman? More than Peter loves his fellow disciples? More than the other disciples love me? There is no hint in John that Peter struggles with loyalties to his career or fellow disciples, and it is not likely that Jesus insists on receiving greater love than others, for elsewhere he insists that love for him is embodied in and through love for other disciples. It is far more likely that Jesus gently taunts Peter, for it was Peter who put himself forward with a promise to follow Jesus to the point of death (13:37), a promise he failed to live up to that very night.[16] But Peter drops any pretense of comparison with others in his reply to Jesus, and Jesus drops any note of comparison when he repeats the question, asking simply, "do you love me?" Moreover, in responding, Peter appeals not to the strength of his own love, but to the sureness of Jesus' knowledge of him: "Yes, Lord; you know that I love you . . . you know everything" (vv. 15, 17).

Different Greek verbs for "love" are employed in the questions and responses: *agapaō* and *phileō*—a difference lost in English translation. Some find this significant, arguing that *agapaō* conveys unconditional love and *phileō* a lesser "brotherly" or "sisterly" love. The first two times Jesus asks "do you love me," he uses the verb *agapaō*, and both times Peter responds in the affirmative using *phileō*. The third time Jesus asks the question, however, he too shifts to *phileō*, and Peter responds again using this same verb. Some would argue, then, that Peter does not grasp what Jesus is asking or cannot deliver it, and thus Jesus accommodates Peter the third time around, settling for less. Alternatively, one could argue that by employing both verb forms Jesus is asking Peter if he loves him fully, in every possible way.[17] However, *agapaō* and *phileō* are used interchangeably, as synonyms, elsewhere in the Fourth Gospel (compare 13:23 and 20:2; 10:17 and 5:20; 14:23 and 16:27), and other shifts in terminology in the exchange (e.g., from "feeding" to "tending," and from "lambs" to "sheep") suggest that nothing more than stylistic variation is at play. Thus distinctions between the verbs should not be pressed.

Whatever the case may be, the question is an embarrassing and painful one, for we are told that Peter "felt hurt" that Jesus had to ask it a third time (21:17). But there was reason for Jesus to question Peter's love. Peter had, after all, denied any association with him (18:15–18, 25–27). But as the question "do you love me" is put to Peter three times, Peter responds in the affirmative three times, thereby undoing the denials. Jesus offers the possibility of a new stage in their relationship and an open future, one in which Peter is not only forgiven, but given a fresh challenge, a work to do—indeed, a share in Jesus' own work: "Feed my lambs. . . . Tend my sheep" (vv. 15–17).

It is a blueprint for a vocation in ministry. Some would say it pertains particularly to those who exercise leadership roles within the Christian community and have special responsibility for oversight of its life, and that may be. But love of Jesus is required of every disciple, and all play a role in the care and nurture of the community of faith. Thus what do we learn about ministry from this exchange, about the practice of caring for Jesus' sheep?

For one thing, it is clear that ministry is entrusted to forgiven sinners, less-than-perfect people, who undertake this work "not to earn the forgiveness and acceptance that has already been given, but as a way of expressing gratitude for the gift of grace, and as a way of living the new, resurrected life we have received."[18] Moreover, it is motivated by one important thing above all else: love of Jesus. As N. T. Wright observes,

> Here is the secret of all Christian ministry, yours and mine, lay and ordained, full-time or part-time. It's the secret of everything from being a quiet, back-row member of a prayer group to being a platform speaker at huge rallies and conferences. If you are going to do any single solitary thing as a follower and servant of Jesus, this is what it's built on. Somewhere, deep down inside, there is a love for Jesus, and though (goodness knows) you've let him down enough times, he wants to find that love, to give you a chance to express it, to heal the hurts and failures of the past, and give you new work to do.[19]

So "do you love me?" It is, in John, "the qualifying exam for pastoral ministry"—the question that must be answered before one is entrusted to care for Jesus' sheep.[20] As commentator Mark Allan Powell notes, "Jesus doesn't *just* want his sheep to be fed; he wants his sheep to be fed by someone who loves him."[21] It is also worth noting that Jesus' question is not "do you love my sheep?" Sheep or fellow disciples are not always lovable and whatever love we have for them will not sustain us in ministry. We will not persevere in shepherding tasks unless the love of Christ is our motivation.[22] Ministry is grounded in *that* love—a love that is lived out in the practice of caring for Jesus' sheep.

Moreover, ministry clearly entails doing for others what Jesus has already done for us. Thus it is after breakfast, after feeding Peter, that Jesus calls him to feed other sheep. In the same way, Jesus insisted on washing the feet of his disciples, before exhorting them to wash the feet of others (John 13). Only as we are nourished and tended by Christ are we able to nourish and tend to others. Another Johannine image conveys this same point: Jesus is the vine, and we are the branches who depend completely upon him for life and fruitful endeavor. Indeed, apart from him we can do nothing (15:5c).

The feeding and tending entailed in pastoral ministry surely includes all the means by which the life of the Christian community is nourished, built up, and sustained. As Caleb Oladipo suggests, it involves watching over people, talking to them, gathering them together, visiting them, putting clothes on them, protecting them, guarding them from physical danger, praying with them, listening to them, and helping them in difficult times.[23] To those practices of ministry we could add all the acts of worship, preaching, and teaching by which believers, young and old, are nourished by the bread of life and enabled to grow as disciples of Jesus Christ. The Gospel of John is not the only biblical witness to employ the language of shepherding to describe pastoral ministry, but it does highlight one additional and distinctive mark of the model shepherd found nowhere else: willingness to die for the sheep. Indeed, Jesus identifies himself as the good shepherd on this basis: "I lay down my life for the sheep" (10:14). Those who tend Jesus' sheep will follow his lead, caring regardless of the consequences, and shepherding to the point of death if need be.

Still, shepherding imagery for ministry is not without its problems. As Fernando Segovia has noted, it can introduce a measure of elitism and subservience into communal relations: the shepherd feeds, leads, and tends; the sheep obey and follow. Sadly, as he reminds us, this underside of the metaphor has dominated relations between First World Christians and the Two-Thirds World. Moreover, Segovia points out that service unto death has applied for the most part to sheep rather than shepherds, as the widespread silence and cooperation of the churches in the face of the enslavement of millions of the black peoples of Africa, the decimation of millions of the indigenous peoples of the Americas, and the long period of colonial exploitation and suppression testify.[24]

Given the potential of the metaphor to foster paternalistic, condescending, oppressive relations, it is important to highlight John's careful qualifying of Peter's shepherding role. For one thing, he is an under-shepherd at most, who never takes the place of Jesus or possession of the flock. As Jesus said earlier, "There will be one flock, one shepherd" (10:16). He remains the one true shepherd, and the relationship that believers have directly with him has priority over all others. His instruction to Peter is "tend *my* sheep." Moreover, Jesus emphasizes duties and obligations rather than prerogatives.[25] Peter is charged with "feeding" and "tending" the Lord's sheep, rather than "governing" and "ruling" them. Indeed, shepherding, in the Gospel of John at least, "bears no ruler-like features."[26] It is a leadership style that takes Jesus, the Good Shepherd, as its model, and is thus based on a relationship of mutual trust, rather than on the exercise of authority.[27] As Jesus said, "I know my own and my own know me" (10:14). Good shepherds call their sheep by name, and sheep follow because they know the shepherd's voice. "They will not follow a stranger" (10:3–5). The shepherd's charge, based on mutual trust, is one of service rather than authority[28]—and one of total dedication to the task of caring for the flock, even to the point of death if need be.

We know that Peter proved his love for Jesus in the end by his faithfulness to this calling, for tradition holds that he died a martyr's death by crucifixion, like his Lord. As Peter's threefold qualifying exam for ministry concludes, Jesus alludes to this future destiny, contrasting Peter's present youth and freedom with the kind of death by which he would die: "when you grow old, you will stretch out your hands, and someone else will fasten a belt around you and take you where you do not wish to go" (v. 18). Jesus describes it as a death that, like his own, would glorify God (v. 19). Having addressed Peter's past failure, his present vocation, and his future destiny, Jesus invites Peter's assent: "Follow me" (v. 19). They are words Peter had longed to hear, for earlier, on the night before Jesus' death, when told he could not follow where Jesus was going, Peter had protested, "Lord, why can I not follow you now? I will lay down my life for you" (13:37)—but failed to live up to those words. Now, however, Jesus invites him to follow, and at the end of his life Peter followed him completely as predicted, with an act of love that matched Jesus' own.

Following Jesus to martyrdom, however, is not the calling of every disciple, though the power of that witness continues to manifest itself in the obedience of believers around the world to this day. There are different vocations in ministry, some less dramatic, and our task is to be faithful to the particular calling that God in Christ has given us. As N. T. Wright puts it, "God makes no mistakes in casting," and "part of Christian obedience . . . is knowing that we are called to follow Jesus wherever he leads *us*, not wherever he leads the person next to us."[29] It is the last lesson in ministry that Peter has to learn, when he turns and sees the disciple whom Jesus loved following them and cannot keep from asking, "Lord, what about him?" (v. 21). What will be his destiny? Will he too be asked to follow Jesus to a cross? We do not know whether Peter asks this question out of curiosity, brotherly concern, or collegial jealousy, though who would deny how easily our egos can get in the way of faithfulness to our own callings? It is hard to keep ourselves from measuring our ministries with the endeavors, accomplishments, or destinies of others. Thus Jesus answers bluntly, directing Peter's attention back to his own vocation: "If it is my will that he remain until I come, what is that to you? Follow me!" (v. 22). In short, we ought not to be distracted from our own discipleship by uncalled-for attention to that of another.[30] We have no jurisdiction over the destiny of others, and our concern should be for our own faithfulness. Thus again and again we too need to hear the final exhortation Jesus gives disciples in John, one that echoes his very first: "Follow me!" (1:43; 21:22).

Our final glimpse of the disciple whom Jesus loved provides one last portrait in ministry. His vocation may be quieter than Peter's, and his destiny less dramatic, but they are of enduring importance to the community of faith. Indeed, he is identified as the eyewitness whose testimony stands behind the Gospel of John's story of Jesus—the authenticator of the tradition on which the written Gospel is based. His witness thus inspires and strengthens the community of faith to this day.

He remains a mystery man to the end, as the Fourth Gospel never reveals his identity. At the time John 21 was written, he was either on the verge of death or had recently died, and this was causing consternation, for "the rumor spread in the community that this disciple would not die" (v. 23). This was apparently a misunderstanding of something that Jesus had said, and the narrator pauses to correct it. Some have suggested that the beloved disciple may have been Lazarus, whom Jesus called forth from the tomb (John 11), for there might well have been an expectation that, having been raised, he would not die again. We will never know for sure. But one thing we do know: "we know that his testimony is true" (v. 24), for it still continues to lead disciples to the one who is the way, the truth, and the life and to inspire them for varied ministries in his name.

The Gospel comes to a close with what is, perhaps, the librarian's nightmare: "there are also many other things that Jesus did; if every one of them were written down, I suppose that the world itself could not contain the books that would be written" (v. 25). It is a final note in a chapter that has been described as an "archives of excess": "an excess of fish, an excess of love, an excess of service, and an extravagant excess of stories about Jesus."[31] By means of it, the one who recorded the beloved disciple's witness for posterity humbly acknowledges that he has had to be selective in the telling of the story. But perhaps it is also an acknowledgment that the story continues—that the one who is the Word made flesh continues to be present in the lives and ministries of those who believe in his name. He cannot be confined to any page. Indeed, new stories of his surprising presence among us, and the abundant life he offers, are unfolding every day.

QUESTIONS FOR DISCUSSION OR REFLECTION

Do a dramatic reading of John 21. Assign roles to a narrator, to Jesus, and to Peter. Have the rest of the group read collectively the lines of the disciples. Following the reading, share briefly: What most captures your attention as you hear the story? What questions does it raise for you?

How would you interpret Peter's decision to go fishing? Would you see it as an illustration of "post-Easter decline"? Why, or why not?

How would you interpret Peter's impetuous action of clothing himself before throwing himself into the sea (v. 7)?

What do you make of the fact that the net was full of exactly 153 fish?

John 21 makes a variety of affirmations about the church's mission. Which are most significant to you, and why?

Do you think the use of two different Greek verbs for love (*agapaō* and *phileō*) in Jesus' questioning of Peter is significant?

Why, or why not? In your view, does Jesus accommodate Peter, settling for less?

To whom do you believe the ministry of shepherding is entrusted? Does Jesus' charge to Peter to feed and tend his sheep pertain particularly to those who exercise leadership roles within the church and have special responsibility for its life? Or does it apply to all disciples, in your view?

What, specifically, do you think the tasks of feeding and tending Jesus' sheep entail?

Would you agree with Fernando Segovia that the shepherding imagery for ministry can introduce a measure of elitism and subservience into communal relations? How would you address this hazard?

Who would you identify, along with Peter, as disciples who have followed Jesus to martyrdom? How has the power of their witness impacted you?

Why do you think Peter asks Jesus about the beloved disciple's destiny? What significance does Jesus' response to this inquiry have for your own discipleship?

The beloved disciple remains a mystery man to the end, though there is no lack of speculation as to who he might be. Is he John, the son of Zebedee, as often assumed? Or Lazarus? Is the beloved disciple necessarily male? Is he a real or symbolic figure, an ideal of discipleship? Could it be that the evangelist has deliberately obscured the beloved disciple's identity, in order that we might imagine ourselves in his shoes? What do you think?

What insights do you gain from John 21 about pastoral ministry, the care and nurture of those within the community of faith? Why are they important to you?

How would you describe your own vocation in ministry? Where has Jesus led you?

With whom do you most identify in this chapter and why?

Notes

Introduction

1. Martin Luther, "Preface to the New Testament" (1522, revised 1546), *Martin Luther's Basic Theological Writings*, ed. Timothy F. Lull, 2nd ed. (Minneapolis: Fortress, 2005), 111. See also Luther, *Word and Sacrament*, vol. 1, ed. E. Theodore Bachmann, *Luther's Works* 35 (St. Louis: Concordia, 1960), 361–62.

2. John Calvin, *Commentary on the Gospel According to John*, vol. 1, trans. William Pringle (repr. Grand Rapids: Eerdmans, 1956), 22.

3. Quoted by Robert Kysar in *The Fourth Evangelist and His Gospel: An Examination of Contemporary Scholarship* (Minneapolis: Fortress, 1975), 6.

4. Robert Kysar has characterized John as a "maverick Gospel" in his fine overview of John's theology entitled *John: The Maverick Gospel*, rev. ed. (Louisville: Westminster/John Knox, 1993).

5. Gail R. O'Day, "John," in *The Women's Bible Commentary*, ed. Carol A. Newsom and Sharon H. Ringe (Louisville: Westminster/John Knox, 1992), 293.

Chapter 1: The Word Became Flesh

1. Wes Howard-Brook, *John's Gospel and the Renewal of the Church* (Maryknoll, N.Y.: Orbis, 1997), 8.

2. Robert Kysar, *John: The Maverick Gospel*, rev. ed. (Louisville: Westminster/John Knox, 1993), 31.

3. Ibid., 32.

4. Fred B. Craddock, *The Gospels*, Interpreting Biblical Texts (Nashville: Abingdon, 1981), 133.

5. The one other reference to Jesus as the "Word of God" is found in Rev. 19:13.

6. Howard-Brook, *John's Gospel*, 2.

7. Kysar, *John: The Maverick Gospel*, 30.

8. I am indebted to Jack Dean Kingsbury for this observation: Kingsbury, "The Gospel in Four Editions," in *Interpreting the Gospels*, ed. James Luther Mays (Philadelphia: Fortress, 1981), 37.

9. Gail R. O'Day, "The Gospel of John," in *The New Interpreter's Bible*, ed. Leander E. Keck, vol. 9 (Nashville: Abingdon, 1995), 524.

10. Ibid., 525–26.

11. Ibid.

12. Saint Augustine, *Confessions*, trans. Henry Chadwick (Oxford: Oxford University Press, 1991), I, i1.

13. Raymond E. Brown, *A Retreat with John the Evangelist: That You May Have Life* (Cincinnati: St. Anthony Messenger Press, 1998), 24.

14. Ibid., 36–37.

15. Ibid., 37.

16. Sandra M. Schneiders, *Written That You May Believe: Encountering Jesus in the Fourth Gospel*, rev. ed. (New York: Crossroad, 2003), 49.

17. Brian A. Wren, *What Language Shall I Borrow? God-Talk in Worship: A Male Response to Feminist Theology* (New York: Crossroad, 1989), 83.

18. Gail R. O'Day, "John," in *The Women's Bible Commentary*, ed. Carol A. Newsom and Sharon H. Ringe (Louisville: Westminster/John Knox, 1992), 304.

19. Ibid.

20. Frederick Buechner, *Wishful Thinking: A Theological ABC* (New York: Harper & Row, 1973), 43.

21. Kathleen Norris, *Amazing Grace: A Vocabulary of Faith* (New York: Riverhead Books, 1998), 31.

Chapter 2: Entrance and Exit Points

1. Gail R. O'Day, "The Gospel of John," in *The New Interpreter's Bible*, ed. Leander E. Keck, vol. 9 (Nashville: Abingdon, 1995), 537.

2. Ibid., 538.

3. Beverly Roberts Gaventa, *Mary: Glimpses of the Mother of Jesus* (Columbia, S.C.: University of South Carolina Press, 1995), 80.

4. Ibid.

5. Ibid., 82.

6. Ibid., 91.

7. Craig R. Koester, *Symbolism in the Fourth Gospel: Meaning, Mystery, Community*, 2nd ed. (Minneapolis: Fortress, 2003), 241.

8. Diana Garland, "What Is Family Ministry?" *Christian Century* 113 (November 13, 1996): 1100–1101.

9. Gail R. O'Day, "John," in *The Women's Bible Commentary*, ed. Carol A. Newsom and Sharon H. Ringe (Louisville: Westminster/John Knox, 1992), 304.

10. David Rhoads, Joanna Dewey, and Donald Michie, *Mark as Story: An Introduction to the Narrative of a Gospel*, 2nd ed. (Minneapolis: Fortress, 1999), 78.

11. R. Alan Culpepper makes this point and provides this quotation in *The Gospel and Letters of John*, Interpreting Biblical Texts (Nashville: Abingdon, 1998), 130. The medieval quotation is a paraphrase of *Epigrammata Sacra*.

Aquae in Vinum Versae, trans. Richard Crashaw (1612?–1649); cf. *The Oxford Dictionary of Quotations*, 3rd ed. (Oxford: Oxford University Press, 1979), 169.

12. O'Day, "John," 295.

Chapter 3: A Clandestine Encounter

1. See Jouette M. Bassler, "Mixed Signals: Nicodemus in the Fourth Gospel," *Journal of Biblical Literature* 108 (1989): 635–46.

2. A. D. Nuttall, *Overheard by God: Fiction and Prayer in Herbert, Milton, Dante, and Saint John* (New York: Methuen, 1980), 131.

3. Frederick Buechner, "Nicodemus," in *Beyond Words: Daily Readings in the ABC's of Faith* (New York: HarperCollins, 2004), 285.

4. Sandra M. Schneiders, *Written That You May Believe: Encountering Jesus in the Fourth Gospel*, rev. ed. (New York: Crossroad, 2003), 121.

5. Tom Wright, *John for Everyone, Part 1: Chapters 1–10* (Louisville: Westminster John Knox, 2004), 30.

6. Francis J. Moloney, "An Adventure with Nicodemus," in *The Personal Voice in Biblical Interpretation*, ed. Ingrid Rosa Kitzberger (London and New York: Routledge, 1999), 102.

7. Gail R. O'Day, "The Gospel of John," in *The New Interpreter's Bible*, ed. Leander E. Keck, vol. 9 (Nashville: Abingdon, 1995), 552.

8. Raymond E. Brown, *The Community of the Beloved Disciple: The Life, Loves, and Hates of an Individual Church in New Testament Times* (New York: Paulist, 1979), 72.

9. Raymond E. Brown, *A Retreat with John the Evangelist: That You May Have Life* (Cincinnati: St. Anthony Messenger Press, 1998), 34.

10. Schneiders, *Written That You May Believe*, 122.

11. Ibid.

12. Ibid., 123.

13. Ibid.

14. Ibid.

15. David Rensberger, *Johannine Faith and Liberating Community* (Philadelphia: Westminster, 1988), 69, 81.

16. Ibid., 114.

17. Ibid., 115.

18. Ibid.

19. Ibid., 116.

20. O'Day, "Gospel of John," 555.

21. Rensberger, *Johannine Faith and Liberating Community*, 40.

22. Craig R. Koester, *Symbolism in the Fourth Gospel*, 2nd ed. (Minneapolis: Fortress, 2003), 229.

23. Gail R. O'Day, "New Birth as a New People: Spirituality and Community in the Fourth Gospel," *Word and World* 8 (Winter 1988): 60.

Chapter 4: Conversation at the Well

1. Fred B. Craddock, "The Witness at the Well," *Christian Century* 107, no. 8 (March 7, 1990): 243.

2. Sandra M. Schneiders, *Written That You May Believe: Encountering Jesus in the Fourth Gospel*, rev. ed. (New York: Crossroad, 2003), 137.

3. Teresa Okure, *The Johannine Approach to Mission: A Contextual Study of John 4:1–42* (Tübingen: Mohr, 1988), 83–86.

4. Gail R. O'Day, *The Word Disclosed: Preaching the Gospel of John*, rev. ed. (St. Louis: Chalice, 2002), 33.

5. On the ambiguity of Nicodemus's subsequent appearances in John's Gospel, see Jouette M. Bassler, "Mixed Signals: Nicodemus in the Fourth Gospel," *Journal of Biblical Literature* 108 (1989): 635–46.

6. Adele Reinhartz, "The Gospel of John," in *Searching the Scriptures*, vol. 2, *A Feminist Commentary*, ed. Elisabeth Schüssler Fiorenza (New York: Crossroad, 1994), 573.

7. Robert Alter, *The Art of Biblical Narrative* (New York: Basic Books, 1981), 50–51.

8. Lyle Eslinger, "The Wooing of the Woman at the Well: Jesus, the Reader and Reader-Response Criticism," *Journal of Literature and Theology* 1 (1987): 167–93; reprinted in *The Gospel of John as Literature: An Anthology of Twentieth-Century Perspectives*, ed. Mark Stibbe (Leiden: Brill, 1993), 165–82.

9. Schneiders, *Written That You May Believe*, 135–36.

10. Craig R. Koester makes this point in *Symbolism in the Fourth Gospel: Meaning, Mystery, Commmunity*, 2nd ed. (Minneapolis: Fortress, 2003), 49.

11. Schneiders, *Written That You May Believe*, 140.

12. See Koester, *Symbolism in the Fourth Gospel*, 49.

13. Schneiders, *Written That You May Believe*, 141.

14. Calvin's interpretation of the Samaritan woman's story is found in his *Commentary on the Gospel According to John*, trans. William Pringle, vol. 1 (Grand Rapids: Eerdmans, 1949), 143–77. These quotations are found on pp. 153 and 168.

15. Gail R. O'Day raises this possibility in her essay on "John" in the *Women's Bible Commentary*, ed. Carol Newsom and Sharon Ringe (Louisville: Westminster/John Knox, 1992), 296.

16. Linda McKinnish Bridges, "John 4:5–42," *Interpretation* 48 (April 1994): 173–76.

17. O'Day, *Word Disclosed*, 47.

18. Ibid.

19. O'Day, "John," 295.

20. See Okure, *Johannine Approach to Mission*, 96–98, for a discussion of interpretive possibilities. Okure argues that Jesus himself is the gift of God (3:16), though others note that 7:37–39 equates "rivers of living water" with "the Spirit." I see no reason that both the gift (Jesus) and the medium by which the new life available in him is received (the Spirit) cannot be in view.

21. O'Day, "John," 296.

22. Raymond E. Brown, *The Gospel according to John (1–XII)*, Anchor Bible (Garden City, N.Y.: Doubleday, 1966), 176.

23. Schneiders, for example, identifies it as such (*Written That You May Believe*, 141).

24. See Gail R. O'Day, *Revelation in the Fourth Gospel* (Philadelphia: Fortress, 1986), 75.

25. Craddock, "Witness at the Well," 243.

26. Schneiders, *Written That You May Believe*, 145.

27. Calvin, *Commentary on John*, 176.

28. Robert Kysar, *John*, Augsburg Commentary on the New Testament (Minneapolis: Augsburg, 1986), 70.

29. Robert Kysar, *John: The Maverick Gospel*, rev. ed. (Louisville: Westminster/John Knox, 1993), 151.

30. Luise Schottroff notes this possibility in "The Samaritan Woman and the Notion of Sexuality in the Fourth Gospel," in *What Is John?"*, vol. 2, *Literary and Social Readings of the Fourth Gospel*, ed. Fernando F. Segovia (Atlanta: Scholars Press, 1998), 165–66.

31. R. Alan Culpepper, *Anatomy of the Fourth Gospel: A Study in Literary Design* (Philadelphia: Fortress, 1983), 192.

Chapter 5: Images of Life

1. Robert Kysar, *John: The Maverick Gospel*, rev. ed. (Louisville: Westminster/John Knox, 1993), 48.

2. Craig R. Koester, *Symbolism in the Fourth Gospel: Meaning, Mystery, Community*, 2nd ed. (Minneapolis: Fortress, 2003), 2.

3. Kysar, *John: The Maverick Gospel*, 89.

4. Craig R. Koester, *Symbolism in the Fourth Gospel: Meaning, Mystery, Community* (Minneapolis: Fortress, 1995), 98.

5. Koester, *Symbolism in the Fourth Gospel*, 2nd ed., 161.

6. James P. Martin, "John 10:1–10," *Interpretation* 32 (April 1978): 174.

7. Ibid., 175.

8. Wes Howard-Brook, *Becoming Children of God: John's Gospel and Radical Discipleship* (Maryknoll, N.Y.: Orbis, 1994), 315.

9. Craig R. Koester, "Jesus the Way, the Cross, and the World according to the Gospel of John," *Word and World* 21 (Fall 2001): 364–65.

10. Gail R. O'Day, "The Gospel of John," in *The New Interpreter's Bible*, ed. Leander E. Keck, vol. 9 (Nashville: Abingdon, 1995), 744–45.

11. Ibid., 744.

12. Ibid., 745.

13. David Rensberger, "Sectarianism and Theological Interpretation in John," in *"What Is John?"*, vol. 2, *Literary and Social Readings of the Fourth Gospel*, ed. Fernando F. Segovia (Atlanta: Scholars Press, 1998), 145–46.

14. O'Day, "Gospel of John," 743–44. While reference to God as Father is a distinctive feature of Christian faith, it is not unique, for Jews also refer to God as Father (see Jer. 3:4; Isa. 64:8).

15. R. Alan Culpepper, "The Gospel of John as a Document of Faith in a Pluralistic Culture," in *"What Is John?"*, vol. 1, *Readers and Readings of the Fourth Gospel*, ed. Fernando F. Segovia (Atlanta: Scholars Press, 1996), 123–24.

16. Raymond E. Brown, *The Churches the Apostles Left Behind* (New York: Paulist, 1984), 86.

17. Ibid.

18. Gail R. O'Day, "John," in *The Women's Bible Commentary*, ed. Carol Newsom and Sharon Ringe (Louisville: Westminster/John Knox, 1992), 303.

Chapter 6: Between a Rock and a Hard Place

1. This point has been persuasively argued by Gail R.O'Day, "John 7:53–8:11: A Study in Misreading," *Journal of Biblical Literature* 111 (1992): 631–40; see also Raymond E. Brown, *The Gospel according to John (I–XII)*, Anchor Bible (Garden City, N.Y.: Doubleday, 1966), 335.

2. In the fifth century, for example, Augustine observed that "certain persons of little faith, or rather enemies of the true faith, fearing, I suppose, lest their wives should be given impunity in sinning, removed from their manuscripts the Lord's act of forgiveness toward the adulteress, as if He who had said 'sin no more' had granted permission to sin" ("Adulterous Marriages" [2.7], trans. Charles T. Huegelmeyer, in *Augustine's Treatises on Marriage and Other Subjects*, trans. Charles T. Wilcox [and others]; ed. Roy J. Deferrari [New York: Fathers of the Church, 1955], 107).

3. Brown, *Gospel according to John*, 336–37.

4. O'Day, "John 7:53–8:11," 633.

5. Ibid.

6. Ibid., 636.

7. Patricia Klindienst Joplin, "Intolerable Language: Jesus and the Woman Taken in Adultery," in *Shadow of Spirit: Postmodernism and Religion*, ed. Philippa Berry and Andrew Wernick (New York: Routledge, 1992), 232.

8. Luise Schottroff, *Lydia's Impatient Sisters: A Feminist Social History of Early Christianity* (Louisville: Westminster John Knox, 1995), 184.

9. Rowan Williams, *Writing in the Dust: After September 11* (Grand Rapids: Eerdmans, 2002), 78.

10. Ibid.

11. Joplin, "Intolerable Language," 232.

12. Ibid., 233.

13. Gail R. O'Day, "The Gospel of John," in *The New Interpreter's Bible*, ed. Leander E. Keck, vol. 9 (Nashville: Abingdon, 1995), 630.

14. O'Day, "John 7:53–8:11," 637.

15. Brad H. Young, "'Save the Adulteress!' Ancient Jewish *Responsa* in the Gospels?" *New Testament Studies* 41 (1995): 59–70.

16. Ibid., 63.

17. Ibid., 65.

18. Ibid.

19. Ibid.

20. Ibid., 67.

21. Ibid., 68.

22. Ibid., 67.

23. Ibid., 69.

24. Ibid., 70.

25. See, for example, Schottroff, *Lydia's Impatient Sisters*, 181. Schottroff claims that "the text reflects a social praxis of getting rid of women by means of accusing them of adultery."

26. See, for example, J. Ian H. McDonald, "The So-Called Pericope *de adultera*," *New Testament Studies* 41 (1995): 420–22. Martin Scott also takes parallels with the Susanna story into account. Indeed, Scott's reading of the story leads him to the conclusion that the woman was not guilty of adultery, but innocent and released from injustice by Jesus ("On the Trail of a Good Story: John 7.53–8.11 in the Gospel Tradition," in *Ciphers in the Sand: Interpretations of the Woman Taken in Adultery (John 7.53–8.11)*, ed. Larry J. Kreitzer and Deborah W. Rooke (Sheffield: Sheffield Academic Press, 2000), 53–82.

27. Jean K. Kim, "Adultery or Hybridity? Reading John 7.53–8.11 from a Postcolonial Context," in *John and Postcolonialism: Travel, Space, and Power*, ed. Musa W. Dube and Jeffrey L. Staley (London: Sheffield Academic Press, 2002), 111–28.

28. Ibid., 125.

29. Ibid., 126.

30. Alan Watson, "Jesus and the Adulteress," *Biblica* 80 (1999): 100–108.

31. Ibid., 102.

32. Ibid., 102–3.

33. Ibid., 107.

34. Ibid., 103.

35. Ibid., 106.

36. Ibid., 107.

37. Ibid., 108.

38. C. Welton Gaddy, *Adultery and Grace: The Ultimate Scandal* (Grand Rapids: Eerdmans, 1996), xii–xiii.

39. Ibid., xiii.

40. Ibid., 155.

41. Roberta C. Bondi, *To Pray and to Love: Conversations on Prayer with the Early Church* (Minneapolis: Fortress, 1991), 109.

42. Ibid., 112. Italics mine.

43. Susan Brooks Thistlethwaite, "Every Two Minutes: Battered Women and

Feminist Interpretation," in *Feminist Interpretation of the Bible*, ed. Letty M. Russell (Philadelphia: Westminster, 1985), 102.

Chapter 7: A Journey to Sight

1. Craig R. Koester, *Symbolism in the Fourth Gospel: Meaning, Mystery, Community*, 2nd ed. (Minneapolis: Fortress, 2003), 161.

2. See Barclay M. Newman and Eugene A. Nida, *A Translator's Handbook on the Gospel of John*, Helps for Translators Series (London and New York: United Bible Societies, 1980), 299; Koester, *Symbolism in the Fourth Gospel*, 105.

3. Guillermo Cook, "Seeing, Judging and Acting: Evangelism in Jesus' Way according to John 9," *Evangelical Review of Theology* 16 (July 1992): 254.

4. Wes Howard-Brook, *Becoming Children of God: John's Gospel and Radical Discipleship* (Maryknoll, N.Y.: Orbis, 1994), 216.

5. Sandra M. Schneiders, *Written That You May Believe: Encountering Jesus in the Fourth Gospel*, rev. ed. (New York: Crossroad, 2003), 151.

6. Ibid., 151, 157.

7. See the groundbreaking work of J. Louis Martyn, which first appeared in 1968, *History and Theology in the Fourth Gospel*, 3rd ed. (Louisville: Westminster John Knox, 2003); and Raymond E. Brown, *The Community of the Beloved Disciple: The Life, Loves, and Hates of an Individual Church in New Testament Times* (New York: Paulist, 1979). The expulsion theory that they put forth has become axiomatic in Johannine studies, though we will consider an important critique of this theory in the following chapter.

8. Martyn, *History and Theology*, 41.

9. Howard-Brook, *Becoming Children of God*, 223.

10. Brown, *Community of the Beloved Disciple*, 41.

11. Raymond E. Brown, *The Gospel according to John (I–XII)*, Anchor Bible (Garden City, N.Y.: Doubleday, 1966), 377.

12. Schneiders, *Written That You May Believe*, 155.

13. Lamar Williamson Jr., *Preaching the Gospel of John: Proclaiming the Living Word* (Louisville: Westminster John Knox, 2004), 114.

14. Howard-Brook, *Becoming Children of God*, 227.

15. Schneiders, *Written That You May Believe*, 158; David Rensberger, *Johannine Faith and Liberating Community* (Philadelphia: Westminster, 1988), 42.

16. Colleen Grant, "Reinterpreting the Healing Narratives," in *Human Disability and the Service of God: Reassessing Religious Practice*, ed. Nancy L. Eiesland and Don E. Saliers (Nashville: Abingdon, 1998), 84.

17. Gail R. O'Day, "The Gospel of John," in *The New Interpreter's Bible*, ed. Leander E. Keck, vol. 9 (Nashville: Abingdon, 1995), 661.

18. Gail R. O'Day, *The Word Disclosed: Preaching the Gospel of John*, rev. ed. (St. Louis: Chalice, 2002), 86.

19. O'Day, "Gospel of John," 664.

20. Ibid.

21. Ibid., 664–65.

22. Craig S. Keener, *The Gospel of John: A Commentary*, vol. 1 (Peabody, Mass.: Hendrickson, 2003), 786–87.

23. Schneiders, *Written That You May Believe*, 122.

24. Ibid., 123.

25. Raymond E. Brown, *A Retreat with John the Evangelist: That You May Have Life* (Cincinnati: St. Anthony Messenger Press, 1998), 46.

26. Ibid., 47.

27. Ibid.

28. Schneiders, *Written That You May Believe*, 161.

29. Brown, *Retreat*, 48.

30. Schneiders, *Written That You May Believe*, 151.

31. Rowan Williams, "Identify Yourself," *Christian Century* 123 (March 21, 2006): 29.

32. Rensberger, *Johannine Faith and Liberating Community*, 45–46.

33. Ibid., 46.

34. Ibid., 46–47.

35. O'Day, *Word Disclosed*, 74–75.

36. John P. Burgess, *Why Scripture Matters: Reading the Bible in a Time of Church Conflict* (Louisville: Westminster John Knox, 1998), 130. Barth's discussion of this matter is found in *Church Dogmatics* II/2, ed. G. W. Bromiley and T. F. Torrance, trans. G. W. Bromiley et al. (Edinburgh: T. & T. Clark, 1957), 717. The quotation from the Second Helvetic Confession comes from chapter XVII, section 5.133 in *The Book of Confessions of the Presbyterian Church (U.S.A.)*.

37. Nancy Eiesland, *The Disabled God: Toward a Liberatory Theology of Disability* (Nashville: Abingdon, 1994), 71.

38. Kathy Black, *A Healing Homiletic: Preaching and Disability* (Nashville: Abingdon, 1996), 43–44.

39. Ibid., 64.

40. Grant, "Reinterpreting the Healing Narratives," 79.

41. Ibid., 81.

42. Black, *Healing Homiletic*, 71.

43. Thanks go to Fritz and Ruth von Fleckenstein of The New York Avenue Presbyterian Church in Washington, D.C., for this insight and for prompting reflection on this final point of connection.

44. Black, *Healing Homiletic*, 70.

45. Ibid., 72.

46. Grant, "Reinterpreting the Healing Narratives," 84.

47. Ibid., 85.

48. Ibid., 85–86.

49. Brown, *Gospel according to John (I–XII)*, 381.

50. Grant, "Reinterpreting the Healing Narratives," 84.

Chapter 8: The Gift of Life

1. An eighth sign is narrated in John 21:1–14. Rightly or wrongly, it is not always included in the list of Jesus' "signs" because chap. 21 is widely regarded as a later addition to John's Gospel.

2. Gail R. O'Day, *The Word Disclosed: Preaching the Gospel of John,* rev. ed. (St. Louis: Chalice, 2002), 103.

3. Gail R. O'Day, "The Gospel of John," in *The New Interpreter's Bible,* ed. Leander E. Keck, vol. 9 (Nashville: Abingdon, 1995), 688.

4. Robert Kysar, *John,* Augsburg Commentary on the New Testament (Minneapolis: Augsburg, 1986), 177.

5. Roberta C. Bondi, *Memories of God: Theological Reflections on a Life* (Nashville: Abingdon, 1995), 33–34.

6. Ibid., 43–44.

7. See chapter 6 of David Rhoads, *The Challenge of Diversity: The Witness of Paul and the Gospels* (Minneapolis: Fortress, 1996), for an excellent discussion of these points and their significance for contemporary Christian life.

8. Both Fred B. Craddock and Gail R. O'Day eloquently make this point. See Craddock, *The Gospels,* Interpreting Biblical Texts (Nashville: Abingdon, 1981), 141; and O'Day, "Gospel of John," 695.

9. Craddock, *Gospels,* 141.

10. Henry David Thoreau, *The Bluebird Carries the Sky on His Back* (Los Angeles: Stanyan Books, 1970).

11. Robert Kysar, *John: The Maverick Gospel,* rev. ed. (Louisville: Westminster/John Knox, 1993), 151.

12. Rabbinic writings that mention this belief are referenced by O'Day, "Gospel of John," 687; Raymond E. Brown, *The Gospel according to John (I–XII),* Anchor Bible (Garden City, N.Y.: Doubleday, 1966), 424; and Craig S. Keener, *The Gospel of John: A Commentary,* vol. 2 (Peabody, Mass.: Hendrickson, 2003), 848 n.123.

13. Craddock, *Gospels,* 141.

14. Adele Reinhartz, *Befriending the Beloved Disciple: A Jewish Reading of the Gospel of John* (New York: Continuum, 2001), 46.

15. Robert Kysar, *Voyages with John: Charting the Fourth Gospel* (Waco: Baylor University Press, 2005), 240.

Chapter 9: The Anointing and Washing of Feet

1. Fred B. Craddock, *John,* Knox Preaching Guides (Atlanta: John Knox, 1982), 91.

2. Ibid.

3. Gail R. O'Day, "John," in *The Women's Bible Commentary,* ed. Carol Newsom and Sharon Ringe (Louisville: Westminster/John Knox, 1992), 299.

4. Craddock, *John,* 100.

5. Robert Kysar, *John*, Augsburg Commentary on the New Testament (Minneapolis: Augsburg, 1986), 208.

6. Craddock, *John*, 101.

7. Kysar, *John*, 209.

8. Gail R. O'Day, "The Gospel of John," in *The New Interpreter's Bible*, ed. Leander E. Keck, vol. 9 (Nashville: Abingdon, 1995), 727.

9. Marianne Meye Thompson, "'His Own Received Him Not': Jesus Washes the Feet of His Disciples," in *The Art of Reading Scripture*, ed. Ellen F. Davis and Richard B. Hays (Grand Rapids: Eerdmans, 2003), 273.

10. Ibid.

11. Wes Howard-Brook, *John's Gospel and the Renewal of the Church* (Maryknoll, N.Y.: Orbis, 1997), 97.

12. Ibid.

13. Ibid., 98.

14. Frederick Buechner, *Wishful Thinking: A Theological ABC* (New York: Harper & Row, 1973), 27.

15. Raymond E. Brown, *The Churches the Apostles Left Behind* (New York: Paulist, 1984), 88 n.128.

16. Sandra M. Schneiders, *Written That You May Believe: Encountering Jesus in the Fourth Gospel*, rev. ed. (New York: Crossroad, 2003), 192.

17. Ibid.

18. Ibid., 193.

19. Ibid.

20. Ibid., 193–94.

21. Ibid., 194.

22. Ibid., 195.

23. Ibid.

24. Thompson, "'His Own Received Him Not,'" 273.

25. Schneiders, *Written That You May Believe*, 195.

26. Ibid.

27. Howard-Brook, *John's Gospel and Renewal*, 99–100.

28. Tom Wright, *John for Everyone, Part 2: Chapters 11–21* (Louisville: Westminster John Knox, 2004), 48.

29. O'Day, "John," 299.

30. Buechner, *Wishful Thinking*, 27.

31. Brown, *Churches the Apostles Left Behind*, 88 n.128.

Chapter 10: Farewell Conversations

1. Fred B. Craddock, *John*, Knox Preaching Guides (Atlanta: John Knox, 1982), 98.

2. Ibid., 97.

3. Henri J. M. Nouwen, *Bread for the Journey: A Daybook of Wisdom and Faith* (HarperSanFrancisco, 1997), June 16.

4. Gail R. O'Day, "John," in *The Women's Bible Commentary*, ed. Carol Newsom and Sharon Ringe (Louisville: Westminster/John Knox, 1992), 302.

5. Raymond E. Brown, *The Churches the Apostles Left Behind* (New York: Paulist, 1984), 106.

6. Ibid., 107.

7. O'Day, "Gospel of John," 777.

8. Raymond E. Brown, "Diverse Views of the Spirit in the New Testament," *Worship* 57 (May 1983): 233.

9. O'Day, "Gospel of John," 754.

10. See Robert Kysar for a clear explication of this point and of John's understanding of the term "world": *John: The Maverick Gospel*, rev. ed. (Louisville: Westminster/John Knox, 1993), 61–65.

11. Kathleen Norris, *Amazing Grace: A Vocabulary of Faith* (New York: Riverhead Books, 1998), 158.

12. Kysar, *John: The Maverick Gospel*, 115.

13. Nouwen, *Bread for the Journey*, June 16.

14. Brown, *Churches the Apostles Left Behind*, 121–22.

Chapter 11: Sovereign in Life and Death

1. Raymond E. Brown, *A Crucified Christ in Holy Week: Essays on the Four Gospel Passion Narratives* (Collegeville, Minn.: Liturgical Press, 1986), 70–71.

2. See John 12:27; 18:11; 19:28; cf. Mark 14:32–42 and Luke 22:39–46.

3. David Rensberger, *Johannine Faith and Liberating Community* (Philadelphia: Westminster, 1988), 91.

4. Wes Howard-Brook, *Becoming Children of God: John's Gospel and Radical Discipleship* (Maryknoll, N.Y.: Orbis, 1994), 392.

5. Cf. Matt. 26:63; 27:14; Mark 14:61; 15:4–5; Luke 23:9.

6. Raymond E. Brown, *The Gospel according to John (XIII–XXI)*, Anchor Bible (Garden City, N.Y.: Doubleday, 1970), 859.

7. Raymond E. Brown, "The Johannine World for Preachers," *Interpretation* 43 (January 1989): 59–60.

8. Gail R. O'Day, "The Gospel of John," in *The New Interpreter's Bible*, ed. Leander E. Keck, vol. 9 (Nashville: Abingdon, 1995), 819–20.

9. Tom Wright, *John for Everyone, Part 2: Chapters 11–21* (Louisville: Westminster John Knox, 2004), 120.

10. See Wayne A. Meeks, *The Prophet King: Moses Traditions and the Johannine Christology* (Leiden: E. J. Brill, 1967), 77, citing *b. Pesaḥ.* 118a.

11. Lamar Williamson Jr., *Preaching the Gospel of John: Proclaiming the Living Word* (Louisville: Westminster John Knox, 2004), 260.

12. Brown, *Gospel according to John (XIII–XXI)*, 858.

13. Ibid., 864.

14. Rensberger, *Johannine Faith and Liberating Community*, 92.

15. Brown, *Gospel according to John (XIII–XXI)*, 864. See also R. Alan Culpepper, *Anatomy of the Fourth Gospel* (Philadelphia: Fortress, 1983), 142–43.

16. See Rensberger, *Johannine Faith and Liberating Community,* 92. See 92–95 for his intriguing interpretation along these lines.

17. Brown, *Crucified Christ in Holy Week*, 60.

18. Rensberger, *Johannine Faith and Liberating Community,* 95.

19. O'Day, "Gospel of John," 814.

20. Ibid.

21. Rensberger, *Johannine Faith and Liberating Community*, 98.

22. Ibid., 99.

23. Ibid., 100.

24. Fred B. Craddock, *John*, Knox Preaching Guides (Atlanta: John Knox, 1982), 134.

25. Cf. Mark 15:34; Matt. 27:46.

26. Brown, *Crucified Christ in Holy Week*, 66.

27. Ibid.

28. Ibid., 67.

29. Ibid., 71.

30. Raymond E. Brown, *The Death of the Messiah: From Gethsemane to the Grave: A Commentary on the Passion Narratives in the Four Gospels,* Anchor Bible Reference Library, 2 vols. (New York: Doubleday, 1994), 1:35.

31. O'Day, "Gospel of John," 837.

32. Robert Kysar, *John: The Maverick Gospel*, rev. ed. (Louisville: Westminster/ John Knox, 1993), 53–54.

33. For example, Rensberger, *Johannine Faith and Liberating Community*, 94.

34. Brown, *Crucified Christ in Holy Week*, 71.

35. Ibid.

Chapter 12: Encounters with the Risen Lord

1. Fred B. Craddock, *John*, Knox Preaching Guides (Atlanta: John Knox, 1982), 142.

2. Ibid., 143.

3. Jane Schaberg, "How Mary Magdalene Became a Whore," *Bible Review* 8 (October 1992): 32.

4. Susan Haskins, *Mary Magdalen: Myth and Metaphor* (New York: Harcourt Brace, 1993), 3–4.

5. See Sandra M. Schneiders, *Written That You May Believe: Encountering Jesus in the Fourth Gospel*, rev. ed. (New York: Crossroad, 2003), 209.

6. Ibid., 207–10.

7. Sandra Schneiders makes this observation in her fine study of this scene: "John

20:1–18: The Encounter of the Easter Jesus with Mary Magdalene—A Transformative Feminist Reading," in *What Is John?"*, vol. 1, *Readers and Readings of the Fourth Gospel*, ed. Fernando F. Segovia (Atlanta: Scholars Press, 1996), 155–68. This essay is reprinted in Sandra M. Schneiders, *Written That You May Believe*, 211–23.

8. Schneiders, *Written That You May Believe*, 218–19.

9. Gail R. O'Day, *The Word Disclosed: John's Story and Narrative Preaching* (St. Louis: CBP Press, 1987), 103.

10. Ibid.

11. Ibid.

12. Ibid., 104.

13. Rowan Williams, "'Do Not Cling to Me,'" *Sojourners Magazine* 32 (July–August 2003): 32–33, 46.

14. Schneiders, *Written That You May Believe*, 220.

15. Mary Rose D'Angelo, "Reconstructing 'Real' Women in Gospel Literature: The Case of Mary Magdalene," in *Women and Christian Origins*, ed. Ross Shepard Kraemer and Mary Rose D'Angelo (New York: Oxford University Press, 1999), 111, 122.

16. Schneiders, *Written That You May Believe*, 215.

17. Ibid., 223.

18. Robert Kysar, *John: The Maverick Gospel*, rev. ed. (Louisville: Westminster/John Knox, 1993), 152.

19. Wes Howard-Brook, *Becoming Children of God: John's Gospel and Radical Discipleship* (Maryknoll, N.Y.: Orbis, 1994), 456.

20. Kysar, *John: The Maverick Gospel*, 121.

21. Raymond E. Brown, *A Risen Christ in Eastertime: Essays on the Gospel Narratives of the Resurrection* (Collegeville, Minn.: Liturgical Press, 1991), 75–76.

22. Mortimer Arias and Alan Johnson, *The Great Commission: Biblical Models for Evangelism* (Nashville: Abingdon, 1992), 79–97.

23. Ibid., 93.

24. Kysar, *John: The Maverick Gospel*, 115.

25. Raymond E. Brown, *The Churches the Apostles Left Behind* (New York: Paulist, 1984), 106.

26. Reginald Fuller, "John 20:19–23," *Interpretation* 32 (April 1978): 183.

27. Craig R. Koester, *Symbolism in the Fourth Gospel: Meaning, Mystery, Community*, 2nd ed. (Minneapolis: Fortress, 2003), 72.

28. Barbara Brown Taylor, *Home by Another Way* (Boston: Cowley, 1999), 114.

29. Wellford Hobbie, *Easter*, Proclamation 3: Aids for Interpreting the Lessons of the Church Year, Series C (Philadelphia: Fortress, 1986), 26–27.

30. Ibid., 27.

31. Luke Timothy Johnson, *The Writings of the New Testament: An Introduction* (Philadelphia: Fortress, 1986), 497.

32. Tom Wright, *John for Everyone, Part 2: Chapters 11–21* (Louisville: Westminster John Knox, 2004), 152.

33. Robert McAfee Brown, *Reclaiming the Bible: Words for the Nineties* (Louisville: Westminster John Knox, 1994), 86.

34. John C. Wronski, "*Written That You May Believe* Study Guide," in Schneiders, *Written That You May Believe,* 292.

35. Schaberg, "How Mary Magdalene Became a Whore," 37.

Chapter 13: Unfinished Business

1. Fred B. Craddock, *John,* Knox Preaching Guides (Atlanta: John Knox, 1982), 146.

2. Rowan Williams, *Resurrection: Interpreting the Easter Gospel,* rev. ed. (Cleveland: Pilgrim, 2002), 28.

3. Wes Howard-Brook, *Becoming Children of God: John's Gospel and Radical Discipleship* (Maryknoll, N.Y.: Orbis, 1994), 469.

4. Mark Stibbe, *John* (Sheffield: Sheffield Academic Press, 1993), 211.

5. Howard-Brook, *Becoming Children of God,* 472.

6. Craig S. Keener, *The Gospel of John: A Commentary,* vol. 2 (Peabody, Mass.: Hendrickson, 2003), 1230.

7. Craig R. Koester, *Symbolism in the Fourth Gospel: Meaning, Mystery, Community,* 2nd ed. (Minneapolis: Fortress, 2003), 312; Raymond E. Brown, *The Gospel according to John (XIII–XXI),* Anchor Bible (Garden City, N.Y.: Doubleday, 1970), 1074.

8. Brown, *Gospel according to John (XIII–XXI),* 1075.

9. Koester, *Symbolism in the Fourth Gospel,* 312.

10. Teresa Okure, *The Johannine Approach to Mission: A Contextual Study of John 4:1–42* (Tübingen: Mohr, 1988), 219.

11. Ibid., 221.

12. Robert Kysar, *Preaching John* (Minneapolis: Fortress, 2002), 169.

13. Marjorie Suchocki, *The Whispered Word: A Theology of Preaching* (St. Louis: Chalice, 1999), 103.

14. Gail R. O'Day, "The Gospel of John," in *The New Interpreter's Bible,* ed. Leander E. Keck, vol. 9 (Nashville: Abingdon, 1995), 864.

15. John M. Buchanan, "Grace at Breakfast," *Christian Century* 123 (May 2, 2006): 3.

16. Gilbert L. Bartholomew, "Feed My Lambs: John 21:15–19 as Oral Gospel," *Semeia* 39 (1987): 83.

17. Kysar, *Preaching John,* 166.

18. Buchanan, "Grace at Breakfast," 3.

19. Tom Wright, *John for Everyone, Part 2: Chapters 11–21* (Louisville: Westminster John Knox, 2004), 165.

20. Raymond E. Brown, "The Johannine World for Preachers," *Interpretation* 43 (January 1989): 65.

21. Mark Allan Powell, *Loving Jesus* (Minneapolis: Fortress, 2004), 178.

22. Caleb O. Oladipo, "John 21:15–17," *Interpretation* 51 (January 1997): 65.

23. Ibid., 66.

24. Fernando Segovia, "The Final Farewell of Jesus: A Reading of John 20:30–21:25" *Semeia* 53 (1991): 187.

25. Brown, *Gospel according to John (XIII–XXI)*, 1115.

26. Rudolf Schnackenburg, *The Gospel according to St. John*, vol. 2, trans. Kevin Smyth (New York: Crossroad, 1990), 295.

27. Stanley H. Skreslet, *Picturing Christian Witness: New Testament Images of Disciples in Mission* (Grand Rapids: Eerdmans, 2006), 176.

28. Okure, *Johannine Approach to Mission*, 224.

29. Wright, *John for Everyone*, 167.

30. Lamar Williamson Jr., *Preaching the Gospel of John: Proclaiming the Living Word* (Louisville: Westminster John Knox, 2004), 299.

31. Beverly Roberts Gaventa, "The Archive of Excess: John 21 and the Problem of Narrative Closure," in *Exploring the Gospel of John: In Honor of D. Moody Smith,* ed. R. Alan Culpepper and C. Clifton Black (Louisville: Westminster John Knox, 1996) 240–41.

CPSIA information can be obtained
at www.ICGtesting.com
Printed in the USA
LVOW12s0418020217
522956LV00003BA/229/P